YouTube Marketing for Beginners

Beginners

Strategies, Tips, and Proven Techniques to Boost Your Brand, Increase Engagement, and Drive Results in the Digital Era

By Diana Eden

TABLE OF CONTENTS

CHAPTER 1: INTRODUCTION TO YOUTUBE MARKETING

Understanding the Importance of YouTube in the Digital Marketing Landscape

YouTube is an essential component of the digital marketing environment because it provides a high-powered platform that enables individuals and organizations to communicate with many people via video content. YouTube's relevance in digital marketing may be attributed to several causes, including the following:

Massive User Base: YouTube is one of the most popular social media sites in the world, with over 2 billion people checking in monthly.

Advertisers can target a wide range of demographics and niches because of the platform's ability to attract a diversified audience.

Video content is more entertaining and often more remembered than text-based material. This is why video content is the dominant form of Content. YouTube is a dynamic platform that may be used to share stories, demonstrate products, and promote preference for visual material, which can deliver complicated concepts in a style that is easier to comprehend.

Google owns benefits to Search Engine Optimization YouTube, and videos posted on the site often rank highly in search engine results.

It is possible to increase the discoverability of Content by optimizing video titles, descriptions, and tags, ultimately driving organic traffic.

Sharing and Integration on Social Media: Videos uploaded to YouTube may be readily shared across various social media sites, meaning their reach can be expanded.

Cross-promotion may be carried out without interruptions with the integration of various social networks and websites.

Engagement & engagement with Users: YouTube makes it possible for users to engage directly with the audience via comments, likes, and shares.

Businesses can cultivate a feeling of community and connection with their target audience, which may ultimately result in enhanced brand loyalty.

Opportunities to generate Educational material Businesses can utilize YouTube to generate instructional films, product demos, and educational material, therefore positioning themselves as experts in their respective industries.

When customers are exposed to educational information, it helps create trust and credibility.

Options for Monetization: Businesses and individuals that create Content can monetize their YouTube channels via advertisements, sponsorships, and collaborations.

This presents an extra income source and serves as an incentive for investing in high-quality materials.

Availability on Mobile Devices: As the number of people using smartphones continues to rise, YouTube is now readily available on mobile devices, enabling advertisers to communicate with viewers while on the go.

Analytics and Insights: YouTube provides marketers with powerful analytics tools that enable them to monitor the success of their videos, understand their audience's behavior, and make choices based on the data collected.

YouTube provides several different ad forms, such as display, non-skippable, and skippable ads. Due to this variety, marketers can choose the format that will be most successful in achieving their objectives.

YouTube can overcome geographical barriers, enabling companies to access a worldwide audience. With YouTube, businesses may also localize their Content.

Marketing professionals can adapt information to a wide variety of consumers by using localization capabilities, which enable them to target certain locations, languages, and demographics.

Collaborations with Influencers: YouTube is a central location for content producers and opinion leaders who have amassed many dedicated followers.

By collaborating with influencers, brands can capitalize on the audiences they already have, thus increasing their reputation and extending their reach.

Opportunities for narrative: The video material found on YouTube provides the option for a captivating narrative, which assists companies in establishing an emotional connection with their audience.

Narratives help develop a memorable brand image, which in turn helps establish a stronger relationship with customers.

It is possible to communicate with the audience in real-time via live streaming, which is made possible by YouTube Live's live streaming capabilities.

Building enthusiasm and engagement via live events, question-and-answer sessions, and product introductions is possible.

The value of Content over the long term is shown by the fact that YouTube videos have a longer shelf life than certain social media postings, which have a shorter lifetime.

Evergreen Content is material that continues to draw views and interaction over a prolonged period, delivering value to marketing efforts over another length of time.

Various Content Types: YouTube is capable of supporting a wide variety of content types, such as tutorials, vlogs, interviews, reviews, and entertainment videos.

Marketers might experiment with various forms to determine which format is most likely to connect with their target audience.

Testimonials and Reviews from Customers: Businesses can present customer testimonials and reviews via video material, which helps to develop trust and authenticity.

Videos uploaded to YouTube that feature pleasant encounters help to a favorable picture of the company.

Instructional and Educational material: Users looking for knowledge and solutions are the target audience for instructional videos and educational material.

A company may establish itself as an expert in its field by establishing itself as a provider of instructional information on its website.

YouTube videos may be integrated into websites and shared across various digital platforms, increasing their total online exposure. This is referred to as cross-platform platform integration.

The integration of several platforms contributes to the creation of a unified brand presence.

YouTube Ads Targeting: The advertising platform that YouTube offers offers comprehensive targeting choices that are based on demographics, interests, and behavior while using the internet.

Using targeted communications, marketers can contact certain audience groups, maximizing the use of advertising dollars.

An Analysis of the Influence That YouTube Has Had on Branding and Engagement

For both people and companies, YouTube has significantly influenced the branding and engagement of their products and services. The platform, which was first introduced in 2005, has developed into the second-largest search engine in the world and has become an essential instrument for digital marketing efforts. The following is an overview of the influence that YouTube has had on engagement and branding:

Advertising:

YouTube allows companies to develop a visual identity by providing them with the ability to do so via bespoke channel designs, logos, and components of consistent branding. One may develop a consistent brand image by carefully designing a channel.

Content promotion: Through the use of high-quality films, brands have the opportunity to promote their goods, services, and core values on YouTube. This contributes to the formation of a stronger connection with the audience as well as the creation of a story that revolves around the brand.

Telling a Story: The video material that can be found on YouTube is an extremely effective venue for telling stories. Companies can establish a more personal relationship with their audience by using films to convey their story, purpose, and values online.

YouTube offers a worldwide audience, enabling marketers to communicate with a wide variety of viewers interested in their Content. Because of this worldwide exposure, brand recognition may be increased, and there is a possibility that new markets might be penetrated.

Credibility and Authority: A brand may position itself as an authority in its line of work by producing Content that is both consistent and useful. The audience's trust and credibility may be increased via the use of videos that are both educational and instructive.

Communities may be created around companies with the help of YouTube, a platform that encourages engagement and community building. Viewers can interact with the content through comments, likes, and shares, which helps cultivate a feeling of belonging and loyalty.

Communication in both directions: Through comments, live broadcasts, and community postings, brands can directly interact with their target audience. By fostering more personal contact between the brand and its clients, direct communication helps to nurture that relationship.

User-Generated Content (UGC): Brands can use user-generated Content by encouraging people to produce material linked to their goods or services. Not only does this keep the audience interested, but it also functions as a genuine testimony.

Analytics and Insights: YouTube offers powerful analytics capabilities, which enable marketers to monitor how well their videos are doing on the platform. The audience's behavior and tastes may be better understood using this data, which also helps optimize Content for more interaction.

Partnerships and Collaborations: To broaden their audience reach and connect with new audiences, businesses might form partnerships with other brands or work with influential individuals. In many cases, collaborative work generates better engagement and exposure levels.

Live Streaming: The live streaming function on YouTube makes it possible to connect in real-time. Brands may create a feeling of immediacy and exclusivity by hosting question-and-answer sessions, product debuts, or events.

YouTube offers various video formats, including lessons, reviews, vlogs, cartoons, and more. This is a significant aspect of the brand's content management strategy. Because of this versatility, marketers can experiment with various formats to determine which ones connect most strongly with their audience.

SEO Advantages: Videos uploaded to YouTube can potentially improve a company's search engine optimization (SEO) efforts. Video material that has been optimized may be shown in Google's search results, which increases the total visibility of the website.

Integrated Content Across several channels: Brands can connect their YouTube content across several channels, including social media, websites, and email marketing campaigns. This technique that utilizes many platforms ensures a consistent brand message and more visibility.

CTA stands for "call to action," YouTube allows marketers to include CTAs in their videos. These CTAs may link viewers to websites, goods, or other Content. This function is useful for transforming viewers' attention into involvement that can be put into action.

Monetization Opportunities YouTube provides the ability to monetize video via advertisements, channel subscriptions, and goods shelves for channels that meet the requirements specified by YouTube. This has the potential to add to the sales stream of a brand.

Involvement to:

Community Tab and Notifications: The Community Tab on YouTube channels enables marketers to communicate with their subscribers directly by sharing material such as polls, updates, and other kinds of Content. Through notifications, users are made aware of newly published information, increasing their engagement level.

Iteration and response: Valuable insights may be gained via an immediate response from the audience, which can be acquired through comments and likes. By using this input, brands can improve their content strategy and better match the expectations of their audience.

Educational content: Brands may utilize YouTube to educate their audience about their goods or their industry. Establishing the brand as a competent and helpful resource may be accomplished via the use of instructional material, the display of products, and how-to videos.

Transferability: Videos uploaded to YouTube may be readily transferred to other platforms. Viewers sharing material broadens the brand's reach and brings it into contact with new groups of people who could become consumers.

YouTube Analytics offers comprehensive data on audience demographics, view time, and engagement metrics, which enables users to make decisions based on the Content they consume. Brands may use this information to improve their content strategy and make choices based on the data.

Accessibility on Mobile Devices: YouTube's mobile accessibility means that companies can connect with viewers at any time and from any location, which is becoming more important as they utilize mobile devices. With mobile-friendly Content, it is essential to communicate with consumers who are on the go.

Companies can utilize YouTube to give behind-the-scenes glimpses into their operations, events, or product development.

This may be done via event coverage and behind-the-scenes recordings. This openness helps to cultivate a feeling of sincerity and allows for a stronger connection with the audience.

YouTube's influence on branding and engagement is, in essence, complex. YouTube provides various tools and capabilities that allow businesses to produce captivating content, connect with their audience, and generate significant interactions beyond the platform itself. When it comes to YouTube, successful businesses often use these capabilities to build a loyal and engaged community.

CHAPTER 2: SETTING UP YOUR YOUTUBE CHANNEL

Creating a Compelling Channel Name and Description

Creating a compelling channel name and description on YouTube is crucial for attracting viewers and conveying the essence of your Content. Here's a step-by-step guide to help you:

Channel Name:

1. **Relevance to Content:**
   - Choose a name that reflects the main theme or focus of your channel. It should give potential viewers an idea of what to expect.

1. **Memorability:**
   - Opt for a name that is easy to remember and spell. Avoid complicated or lengthy names that may be difficult for users to recall.

1. **Uniqueness:**
   - Check the availability of the name to ensure it's unique and not already in use by another channel. You want to stand out from the crowd.

1. **Brand Consistency:**
   - If you already have a personal or brand identity, incorporate that into your channel name for consistency across platforms.

1. **Avoid Trends:**
   - While it's tempting to ride on current trends, consider the long-term appeal of your channel name. Trends come and go, but your Content might stay relevant.

Channel Description:

1. **Introduction:**

- Start with a brief and engaging introduction about yourself or your brand. Mention what viewers can expect from your channel.

1. **Content Overview:**

- Clearly outline the type of Content you'll be producing. Be specific about your videos' topics, themes, or genres.

1. **Unique Selling Proposition (USP):**

- Highlight what makes your channel unique. Why should viewers subscribe to your channel? What value do you offer that others don't?

1. **Posting Schedule:**

- If you have a consistent posting schedule, mention it in your description. This sets expectations for your audience and helps in building a regular viewership.

1. **Call-to-Action (CTA):**

- Encourage viewers to subscribe, like, and share your videos. You can also direct them to your other social media platforms or related Content.

1. **Engage with Viewers:**

- Invite viewers to comment on your videos and participate in discussions. Let them know that their opinions and feedback are valued.

1. **Contact Information:**

- Include links to your other social media profiles, website, or relevant contact information. This makes it easier for viewers to connect with you.

1. **Keywords:**

- Use relevant keywords in your description to improve searchability. Think about terms users might use to find Content similar to yours.

Remember to periodically review and update your channel description to reflect any changes in your Content or goals. Consistency and clarity are key to building a strong YouTube presence.

Customizing Your Channel Layout and Branding

Customizing your YouTube channel layout and branding involves using the YouTube Studio. Please note that YouTube's interface and features may have changed since then, so checking the latest YouTube help resources for the most up-to-date information is a good idea. As of my last update, here's a general guide:

Customizing Your YouTube Channel Layout:

1. **Access YouTube Studio:**
   - Log in to your YouTube account.
   - Click on your profile picture in the top right corner.
   - Select "YouTube Studio" from the dropdown menu.

1. **Navigate to the Customization Tab:**
   - Find the left sidebar in YouTube Studio and click "Customization."

1. **Customize Layout:**
   - Under the "Layout" tab, you can arrange the sections on your channel homepage.
   - Drag and drop sections to reorder them as you prefer.

- Click on the pencil icon to edit specific sections.

1. **Add Sections:**
   - To add sections, click on the "+ Add Section" button.
   - Choose from various types of sections like Popular Uploads, Playlists, etc.
   - Customize the settings for each section.

Branding Your YouTube Channel:

1. **Add a Channel Banner:**
   - In the "Customization" tab, click on the "Branding" tab.
   - Upload a channel banner. The recommended size is 2560 x 1440 pixels, with a safe area of 1546 x 423 pixels where text and logos are not cut off on different devices.

1. **Create a Channel Icon:**
   - Your channel icon is a small image associated with your channel. Click "Change" under the channel icon section to upload or change your channel icon.

1. **Channel Description:**
   - Write a compelling channel description. This gives visitors an idea of what your channel is about.

1. **Add Social Links:**
   - You can add links to your social media profiles. Click on "Links" under the "Basic info" tab.

1. **Video Watermark:**
   - You can add a video watermark that appears on all your videos. This can be your logo. Click on "Branding" under the "Settings" tab.

1. **Customize Thumbnails:**

- Make sure to upload custom thumbnails for your videos. Thumbnails can greatly impact click-through rates.

1. **Color Scheme:**
   - Choose a color scheme that complements your brand. This can be done in the "Brand" tab.

1. **Feature Channels:**
   - In the "Customization" tab, you can feature other channels on your channel homepage. This can be a great way to collaborate with other creators.

Advanced Channel Customization:

1. **Channel Trailer:**
   - Consider creating a channel trailer that introduces new visitors to your Content. You can set this up in the "Customization" tab by choosing a video for new visitors.

1. **Featured Sections:**
   - Besides popular uploads and playlists, you can feature specific videos or playlists by creating custom sections. This allows you to curate Content for your audience.

1. **Playlists:**
   - Organize your videos into playlists. Playlists can be featured on your channel, providing an organized way for viewers to explore your Content by theme or topic.

1. **Community Tab:**
   - Utilize the Community tab to interact with your audience. Share updates, polls, and images to engage with your subscribers.

Channel Analytics:

1. **YouTube Analytics:**

   - Dive into YouTube Analytics to understand your audience, their demographics, and the performance of your videos. Use this information to tailor your Content and strategy.

Channel Verification:

1. **Verify Your Channel:**

   - If eligible, consider verifying your channel. This adds a checkmark next to your channel name, signifying authenticity.

Monetization and Merchandising:

1. **Monetization:**

   - If your channel is eligible, you can apply for the YouTube Partner Program (YPP) to monetize your Content through ads.

1. **Merch Shelf:**

   - You can set up a Merch Shelf to showcase and sell products directly from your channel if you have merchandise.

Collaboration and Branding Guidelines:

1. **Collaborations:**

   - Collaborate with other creators. You can showcase these collaborations on your channel to cross-promote Content and build a community.

1. **Branding Guidelines:**

   - Develop consistent branding elements such as a unique logo, color scheme, and style for your thumbnails to make your channel easily recognizable.

Mobile Optimization:

1. **Check Mobile Appearance:**
   - Ensure your channel banner, thumbnails, and other elements are optimized for mobile viewing.

SEO Optimization:

1. **Video Titles, Descriptions, and Tags:**
   - Optimize your video titles, descriptions, and tags with relevant keywords to enhance discoverability.

1. **Channel Keywords:**
   - In the "Basic info" section, add relevant channel keywords to help YouTube understand your Content better.

Interaction and Engagement:

1. **Reply to Comments:**
   - Engage with your audience by responding to comments on your videos. This helps build a sense of community.

1. **Live Streaming:**
   - Consider using live streams to interact with your audience in real time. YouTube often prioritizes live Content.

1. **Community Posts:**
   - Use the Community tab to share behind-the-scenes content and updates or ask for feedback.

Accessibility:

1. **Closed Captions:**
   - Add closed captions to your videos to make them more accessible to a wider audience.

These are some additional aspects you can consider when customizing your YouTube channel. Remember that YouTube's features and policies may evolve, so regularly check their official resources for the latest information.

CHAPTER 3: CRAFTING ENGAGING CONTENT

Identifying Your Target Audience

Identifying your target audience on YouTube is crucial in creating Content that resonates with the right people. Here are some steps to help you identify and understand your target audience on YouTube:

1. **Define Your Niche:**
   - Clearly define the niche or topic of your YouTube channel. Knowing your niche will help you narrow down your target audience.

1. **Research Your Competitors:**
   - Identify other YouTube channels in your niche. Analyze their Content and audience engagement to understand who is already interested in similar Content.

1. **Use YouTube Analytics:**
   - Take advantage of YouTube Analytics to gather data about your existing audience. Look at demographics, geography, and interests to identify patterns. This data can provide valuable insights into the characteristics of your current audience.

1. **Engage with Your Viewers:**

- Pay attention to the comments section and engage with your viewers. Ask questions, encourage discussions, and seek feedback. This can help you understand the interests and preferences of your audience.

1. **Create Viewer Personas:**

    - Develop detailed personas representing your ideal viewers. Consider age, gender, location, interests, and online behavior. This will help you tailor your Content to meet the needs of your target audience.

1. **Use Social Media:**

    - Leverage other social media platforms to connect with your audience. Platforms like Instagram, Twitter, and Facebook can provide additional insights into the demographics and interests of your viewers.

1. **Conduct Surveys and Polls:**

    - Use YouTube community posts or external survey tools to gather direct feedback from your audience. Ask questions about their preferences, interests, and expectations to refine your content strategy.

1. **Monitor Trends:**

    - Stay informed about trending topics within your niche. This will not only help you create relevant Content but also attract viewers who are interested in popular trends.

1. **Optimize Titles and Thumbnails:**

    - Craft titles and thumbnails that are appealing to your target audience. Pay attention to the language and visual elements that resonate with them.

1. **Track Performance Metrics:**

- Regularly monitor the performance of your videos. Pay attention to metrics like watch time, click-through rate, and engagement. Analyzing this data can help you identify which Content is most popular among your target audience.

1. **Collaborate with Others in Your Niche:**

   - Collaborating with other YouTubers in your niche can expose your Content to a wider audience. Pay attention to the audience overlap and engage with the new viewers to understand their preferences.

1. **Monitor Search Trends:**

   - Use tools like Google Trends or YouTube search trends to identify popular topics within your niche. Creating Content around trending topics can attract a larger audience interested in current discussions.

1. **Host Q&A Sessions:**

   - Conduct regular Q&A sessions where your audience can ask questions. This helps you understand their concerns and interests and fosters a sense of community.

1. **Utilize Hashtags:**

   - Incorporate relevant hashtags in your video descriptions and social media promotions. This can help your videos get discovered by users searching for Content related to those hashtags.

1. **Diversify Content Formats:**

   - Experiment with different content formats such as tutorials, vlogs, interviews, or behind-the-scenes footage. Assess which formats resonate most with your audience and tailor your content strategy accordingly.

1. **Encourage Subscriptions and Notifications:**
   - Remind viewers to subscribe to your channel and enable notifications. This can help you build a more dedicated audience that doesn't miss your new Content.

1. **Attend Industry Events:**
   - Attend relevant events, conferences, or meetups within your niche. Networking with people in your industry can provide valuable insights and help you understand your target audience better.

1. **Offer Incentives:**
   - Consider offering incentives such as exclusive Content, giveaways, or discounts for your subscribers. This can help build loyalty and keep your audience engaged.

1. **Adapt to Feedback:**
   - Act on feedback from your audience. If viewers provide suggestions or express preferences, be open to adapting your content strategy based on their input.

1. **Stay Consistent:**
   - Consistency in posting schedule and content style is key. It helps build trust with your audience; they'll know what to expect from your channel. This consistency can contribute to audience retention.

Remember that the YouTube landscape is dynamic, and audience preferences may evolve. Regularly reassess and adjust your strategy to stay connected with your target audience on YouTube.

Planning and Creating High-Quality Videos

Creating high-quality videos for YouTube involves careful planning, attention to detail, and focusing on delivering value to your audience. Here are some steps and tips to help you plan and create compelling YouTube videos:

1. Define Your Purpose and Audience:

- Identify the purpose of your channel (entertainment, education, tutorials, etc.).
- Understand your target audience and tailor your Content to meet their needs.

2. Research and Keyword Planning:

- Conduct keyword research to understand what your audience is searching for.
- Use tools like Google Keyword Planner, YouTube's search suggest feature, or dedicated keyword research tools.

3. Scripting and Storyboarding:

- Plan your Content with a script or outline to ensure a logical flow.
- Create a storyboard to visualize the scenes and shots in your video.

4. Invest in Good Equipment:

- Use a high-quality camera for recording (DSLRs, mirrorless, or high-end smartphones).
- Invest in a good microphone for clear audio.
- Proper lighting is crucial; consider natural light or invest in studio lights.

5. Set Up a Dedicated Space:

- Create a consistent background or setting for your videos.
- Eliminate background noise and distractions.

6. Create Engaging Thumbnails and Titles:

- Thumbnails and titles should be eye-catching and represent the Content accurately.
- Use high-resolution images and bold, readable text.

7. Editing Software:

- For polished videos, use professional video editing software (e.g., Adobe Premiere Pro, Final Cut Pro, DaVinci Resolve).
- Edit for pacing, removing unnecessary elements, and adding visual appeal.

8. Optimize Video Length:

- Keep videos concise and engaging. Aim for a balance between providing valuable Content and holding viewers' attention.
- Consider breaking long Content into shorter, digestible segments.

9. Optimize Video SEO:

- Optimize video titles, descriptions, and tags with relevant keywords.
- Add a compelling video description that provides additional information and links.

10. Create Consistent Branding:

- Use consistent branding elements such as intros, outros, and watermarks.
- Develop a recognizable visual style for your thumbnails and channel art.

11. Engage with Your Audience:

- Respond to comments on your videos.
- Encourage viewers to like, share, and subscribe.

12. Promote on Other Platforms:

- Share your videos on social media to increase visibility.

- Collaborate with other YouTubers to cross-promote.

13. Analytics and Feedback:

- Monitor YouTube analytics to understand viewer behavior.
- Pay attention to feedback and adjust your Content based on audience preferences.

14. Consistent Upload Schedule:

- Upload videos consistently to build a loyal audience.
- Establish a schedule that works for you and your audience.

15. Stay Informed and Adapt:

- Keep up with YouTube trends and algorithm changes.
- Be willing to adapt your content strategy based on performance and audience feedback.

By focusing on these aspects, you can create high-quality videos that meet YouTube's standards and resonate with your target audience. Consistency and continuous improvement are key to building a successful YouTube channel.

Utilizing Different Types of Content (Tutorials, Vlogs, Reviews, etc.)

Utilizing different types of Content on YouTube can be a powerful strategy to engage your audience and build a strong online presence. Here are some popular types of Content you can consider for your YouTube marketing efforts:

1. **Tutorials:**
   - **Purpose:** Educate your audience on a specific topic or demonstrate how to use a product or service.

- **Tips:** Keep tutorials concise, well-organized, and visually appealing. Use clear and easy-to-follow instructions.

1. **Vlogs:**

    - **Purpose:** Showcase your daily life, behind-the-scenes footage, or share personal experiences to connect with your audience.
    - **Tips:** Be authentic and genuine. Use storytelling, share interesting anecdotes, and maintain a consistent vlogging style.

1. **Reviews:**

    - **Purpose:** Provide your audience insights into products, services, or experiences to help them make informed decisions.
    - **Tips:** Be honest in your reviews, showcase both pros and cons and use high-quality visuals. Compare and contrast different options for added value.

1. **How-to Guides:**

    - **Purpose:** Similar to tutorials but focused on step-by-step guides for specific tasks or achieving particular goals.
    - **Tips:** Clearly outline each step, use visuals or animations for better understanding, and address common challenges or FAQs.

1. **Interviews:**

    - **Purpose:** Bring industry experts, influencers, or interesting personalities for engaging conversations.
    - **Tips:** Choose relevant guests, prepare thoughtful questions, and create a conversational atmosphere. Highlight key takeaways in the video description.

1. **Product Demonstrations:**
   - **Purpose:** Showcase the features and benefits of a product or service.
   - **Tips:** Focus on the unique selling points, demonstrate real-world applications, and address potential concerns or questions.

1. **Q&A Sessions:**
   - **Purpose:** Engage with your audience by answering their questions or addressing common concerns.
   - **Tips:** Collect questions from your audience in advance, keep the session organized, and encourage viewers to participate in future Q&A sessions.

1. **Live Streams:**
   - **Purpose:** Interact with your audience in real-time, answer questions, and provide live Content.
   - **Tips:** Promote live streams in advance, engage with viewers during the stream, and repurpose the Content afterward.

1. **Behind-the-Scenes Content:**
   - **Purpose:** Offer a glimpse into your creative process, workspace, or the making of your Content.
   - **Tips:** Humanize your brand, showcase the people behind the scenes, and provide insights that viewers wouldn't normally see.

1. **Collaborations:**
   - **Purpose:** Collaborate with other YouTubers or influencers to tap into their audience and cross-promote Content.

- **Tips:** Choose collaborators with a similar target audience, plan the collaboration thoroughly, and promote the Content on both channels.

1. **Case Studies:**

   - **Purpose:** Share real-life examples of how your product or service has benefited customers or clients.

   - **Tips:** Include testimonials, metrics, and before-and-after scenarios to highlight the impact.

1. **Educational Series:**

   - **Purpose:** Break down complex topics into educational videos for an in-depth exploration.

   - **Tips:** Plan a structured series with a clear progression, and encourage viewers to watch the entire series for a comprehensive understanding.

1. **Roundup or Compilation Videos:**

   - **Purpose:** Curate and compile Content from various sources to create a comprehensive overview or highlight reel.

   - **Tips:** Provide context for each snippet, credit the original creators, and add your unique insights.

1. **Challenges and Experiments:**

   - **Purpose:** Take on challenges or conduct experiments related to your niche to entertain and engage your audience.

   - **Tips:** Ensure the challenges are relevant, safe, and aligned with your brand. Document the process and share the results.

1. **Documentary-Style Content:**

   - **Purpose:** Create in-depth, narrative-driven Content that explores a specific topic or journey.

- **Tips:** Invest in storytelling, use high-quality visuals, and maintain a captivating narrative throughout.

1. **Product Updates and Announcements:**
   - **Purpose:** Keep your audience informed about new product launches, updates, or significant announcements.
   - **Tips:** Create anticipation through teaser videos, provide detailed information, and address common questions.

1. **Interactive Content:**
   - **Purpose:** Engage viewers with interactive elements, such as polls, quizzes, or choose-your-own-adventure style videos.
   - **Tips:** Encourage audience participation and use interactive features available on YouTube.

1. **Holiday and Seasonal Content:**
   - **Purpose:** Create Content tailored to specific holidays or seasons to stay relevant and tap into trending topics.
   - **Tips:** Plan, be creative with thematic elements, and incorporate holiday-specific promotions or messages.

1. **Motivational or Inspirational Content:**
   - **Purpose:** Inspire and motivate your audience through personal stories, success stories, or uplifting messages.
   - **Tips:** Be authentic, share relatable experiences, and provide actionable advice or takeaways.

1. **Educational Animations:**
   - **Purpose:** Use animated Content to explain complex concepts, processes, or data.

- **Tips:** Ensure animations are clear, visually appealing, and enhance the understanding of the topic.

1. **Flashback or Throwback Videos:**
   - **Purpose:** Share memorable moments from the past, whether personal or related to your brand's journey.
   - **Tips:** Add context to the flashback, reflect on the growth or changes, and invite viewers to share their memories.

Keeping your channel diverse and engaging is crucial. Analyze performance metrics regularly and adjust strategy based on feedback and trends within your niche.

CHAPTER 4: VIDEO SEO BASICS

Optimizing Video Titles, Descriptions, and Tags

When it comes to increasing the exposure and discoverability of your video on YouTube, optimizing your videos' titles, descriptions, and tags is very necessary. The following are some suggestions that can assist you in optimizing these components for efficient marketing on YouTube:

1. Conduct Keyword Research: Using tools such as Google Keyword Planner, SEMrush, or the search suggest option directly offered by YouTube, you should identify relevant terms that are associated with the content of your video.

You may improve your chances of ranking highly by targeting a combination of keywords with high and low levels of competition.

2. Captivating Video Titles:

Make titles that are captivating and represent the film's information in a clear and concise manner.

Ensure that titles are concise and do not exceed the limit of sixty characters to get maximum exposure in search results.

Include the primary keyword in the title at an early stage.

Writing descriptions that are precise, insightful, and rich in keywords (about 200-300 words) is the third step in creating engaging descriptions.

It is important to provide pertinent links (such as social media and websites) and timestamps for the various segments of the video.

You should include a brief overview or hook in the first couple of lines to pique the audience's interest.

4. Tags: Include a variety of general and specialized tags about your video's topic.

Users may utilize phrases and single keywords you have included in your work when looking for similar information.

For optimal coverage, use all of the available tag spaces (about 15-20 tags).

5. Create thumbnails that are visually attractive and appropriately depict your film. This is the fifth step in search engine optimization.

Make use of high-quality photographs and add text and colors that contrast with one another to make them stand out.

Investigate a variety of thumbnail designs to see which are most appealing to your audience.

6. Captivating Intros: To limit the number of people that leave your video without watching it, grab their interest within the first few seconds of the video.

Deliver the value or substance of your film clearly and concisely from the beginning.

Encourage visitors to like, comment, share, and subscribe to your channel using the call to action (CTA) feature.

Both your video and your description should have a call-to-action that is both clear and concise.

8. Interact with Comments: It is important to swiftly respond to comments to encourage member participation in the community and boost the possibility that your video will be recommended.

9. Playlists: Create playlists and organize your films according to the subjects or themes they cover.

Watch time may be increased using playlists, which can keep people on your channel longer.

10. Monitoring Analytics: Make it a habit to check YouTube Analytics regularly to understand how viewers find and interact with your material.

To improve your approach over time, you may use this data.

11. Promote on Other Platforms: To get more traffic, you should embed your videos on your website or blog and share them on social media with your audience.

12. Constant Branding: To have a professional and easily identifiable appearance, it is important to keep your branding and style constant throughout all your channels.

Since this is the thirteenth recommendation, you should provide closed captions or transcriptions for your movies. Not only does this make your material more accessible, but it also assists search engines in comprehending the subjects covered in your movie.

14. Localization: If you have a global audience, you should think about making subtitles or giving translations for the titles, descriptions, and tags of your videos to reach a larger audience.

15. Optimal Video Duration: An ideal video duration corresponds to the level of depth and complexity of the subject you are presenting. The goal is to keep viewers interested throughout the video, although, generally, films that are between seven and fifteen minutes tend to do well.

16. Maintaining a Regular publishing timetable: To create a sense of expectation and dependability among your audience, develop a consistent publishing timetable. Maintaining Consistency may have a beneficial effect on the algorithmic success of your channel.

Create personalized thumbnails visually consistent with your brand and stand out in a crowded search or recommended video stream. Additionally, make sure that your thumbnails are optimized for search engines.

18. Positioning of Keywords: It is crucial to position relevant keywords at the beginning of the titles and descriptions of your videos. This may have a beneficial effect on the ranks of search engines.

19. Playlists for Promotional reasons: Be sure to create playlists tailored exclusively for promotional reasons. These may be your most popular videos, the most recent videos you have uploaded, or videos that revolve around a certain topic.

Utilize YouTube Cards and End Screens: Use the interactive tools that YouTube provides, such as cards and end screens, to promote additional videos, playlists, or direct connections to other websites. Increased overall involvement is a result of this improvement.

You should make compelling thumbnails since thumbnails are often the first thing people see about a website. Please make sure that they are captivating and that they appropriately depict the topic of the film. Experiment with various designs to see which ones are most well-received by your target demographic.

22. Make Use of Information Cards: Include information cards in your videos so that you may give more context or references to stuff that is linked to the video. This both maintains viewers' interest and encourages them to watch other videos from your channel.

23. Collaborate with Other YouTubers: Working with other YouTubers may help you reach a new audience for your YouTube channel. Together with other YouTubers in your field, you may create material that is helpful to both of you.

Monitor Trends: Ensure you are current on the latest trends in your sector or specialized field. The likelihood of your video getting found may be improved by producing material centered on currently popular themes.

Creating Compelling Playlists: Arrange your videos into playlists according to the themes or series you are interested in. This encourages people to watch more of your material, ultimately increasing the total time spent watching.

Invest in high-quality video and audio production since this is the 26th quality and production point. High-quality production can favorably influence the retention and engagement of viewers.

Use YouTube Analytics to your advantage:

Review your YouTube Analytics regularly to better understand your audience, recognize patterns, and improve your content strategy depending on the actions of your viewers.

28. Experiment with Different Titles and Thumbnails: Conduct A/B tests on various titles and thumbnails to see which strongly connect with potential customers. You can test these components using YouTube Studio.

29. Create Compelling Channel Art: The banner and logo you choose for your channel should be visually attractive and reflect your business. Building recognition is facilitated by maintaining a consistent brand.

30. Maintain an Adequate Knowledge of YouTube's Policies:

Maintaining an up-to-date knowledge of YouTube's regulations is essential to prevent any infractions that might harm your channel.

You will be in a better position to optimize your videos for exposure, engagement, and long-term success on YouTube to the extent that you include these extra methods in your marketing activities on YouTube.

Leveraging Thumbnails for Click-Worthy Content

Creating click-worthy content on YouTube involves many factors, and thumbnails are crucial in grabbing viewers' attention. Thumbnails act as the first impression of your video, and they can significantly impact click-through rates. Here are some tips for leveraging thumbnails to make your YouTube content more click-worthy:

1. **High-Quality Images:**
   - Use high-resolution images for your thumbnails to ensure clarity and professionalism.
   - Avoid pixelation or blurriness, as this can make your video appear low-quality.

1. **Consistent Branding:**
   - Maintain a consistent style for your thumbnails to establish a recognizable brand identity.
   - Use a consistent color scheme, fonts, and overall design that align with your brand.

1. **Clear and Bold Text:**
   - Add concise and bold text highlighting your video's key point or value.
   - Use large, readable fonts that stand out even on smaller screens.

1. **Contrasting Colors:**
   - Choose colors that contrast well to make your text and key elements easily visible.

- Consider using complementary colors to make certain elements pop.

1. **Faces and Expressions:**
   - If applicable, include close-ups of faces expressing emotions related to the video content.
   - Humans are naturally drawn to faces, and emotional expressions can capture attention.

1. **Minimalism and Simplicity:**
   - Keep thumbnails simple and uncluttered to avoid overwhelming viewers.
   - Focus on one or two main elements that represent the essence of your video.

1. **Custom Thumbnails:**
   - Avoid using auto-generated thumbnails. Create custom thumbnails tailored to your content.
   - This allows you to control the visual representation of your video and make it more enticing.

1. **Relevance to Content:**
   - Ensure that the thumbnail accurately represents the content of the video.
   - Misleading thumbnails can lead to a negative user experience and harm your channel's credibility.

1. **Test and Analyze:**
   - Experiment with different thumbnail designs to see what resonates best with your audience.
   - Use YouTube analytics to track the performance of different thumbnails and adjust your approach accordingly.

1. **Mobile Optimization:**

- Since many YouTube viewers use mobile devices, ensure your thumbnails are optimized for smaller screens.
- Check the visibility and readability of thumbnails on various devices.

1. **Use Thumbnails as a Storytelling Element:**
   - Create thumbnails that tell a visual story or spark curiosity about the video content.
   - Use images that evoke emotions or intrigue to encourage clicks.

1. **Add Borders and Shadows:**
   - Add subtle borders or shadows around key elements in your thumbnails to make them stand out.
   - This can create a sense of depth and draw attention to important details.

1. **Use Contrasting Fonts:**
   - If your thumbnail includes text, choose fonts that are easy to read and clearly contrast the background.
   - Experiment with different font styles to find the best for your brand and content.

1. **Highlight Benefits or Value:**
   - Showcase the main benefits or value proposition of your video on the thumbnail.
   - Let viewers know what they will gain by clicking on your video.

1. **Overlay Icons or Logos:**
   - Consider adding small overlay icons or logos representing your brand or the video's theme.

- This reinforces brand recognition and adds a professional touch to your thumbnails.

1. **Dynamic Imagery:**

   - Use dynamic and engaging images that convey action or movement.

   - Images with a sense of motion can capture attention and create a sense of excitement.

1. **Emphasize Thumbnails in Series:**

   - If your content is part of a series, maintain Consistency across thumbnails to create a cohesive look.

   - Viewers may be likelier to click on videos they recognize as part of a series they enjoy.

1. **Time-Sensitive Elements:**

   - Consider adding relevant elements to your thumbnail if your video is time-sensitive or related to current events.

   - This can create a sense of urgency and encourage viewers to click sooner rather than later.

1. **Audience Persona Consideration:**

   - Understand your target audience and tailor your thumbnails to resonate with their preferences and interests.

   - The more your thumbnails align with your audience's tastes, the higher the likelihood of engagement.

1. **A/B Testing:**

   - Conduct A/B testing by creating multiple versions of a thumbnail and testing them with a small portion of your audience.

- Analyze the performance metrics to determine which thumbnail design yields better results.

1. **Add Curiosity Hooks:**

   - Pose questions, use intriguing imagery, or include incomplete scenarios in your thumbnails to pique viewers' curiosity.

   - Encourage them to click to find out more.

1. **Utilize YouTube's Official Tools:**

   - Take advantage of YouTube's features, such as adding text and graphics using their built-in tools.

   - This can streamline the thumbnail creation process and ensure compatibility with the platform.

Remember to stay updated on YouTube's guidelines and thumbnail recommendations to ensure compliance with their policies. Regularly analyze your video performance metrics to refine your thumbnail strategy based on audience engagement and feedback. Creating click-worthy thumbnails is an ongoing process of refinement and adaptation to your audience's preferences.

CHAPTER 5: BUILDING A CONTENT CALENDAR

Planning and Scheduling Your Video Releases

Planning and scheduling your video releases on YouTube is crucial for a successful marketing strategy. Consistency and timing play significant roles in building and maintaining an audience. Here's a step-by-step guide to help you plan and schedule your video releases effectively:

1. Understand Your Audience:

- Identify your target audience and their online habits.
- Analyze the best times and days when your audience is most active on YouTube.

2. Create a Content Calendar:

- Develop a content calendar outlining the topics and themes for each video.
- Plan for a mix of content types to keep your channel diverse and interesting.

3. Set a Posting Schedule:

- Determine how often you'll release new videos (daily, weekly, bi-weekly, etc.).
- Consistency is key, so choose a schedule that you can realistically maintain.

4. Consider Video Length and Format:

- Understand the ideal video length for your audience. Some prefer short, snackable content, while others may engage more with longer, in-depth videos.
- Experiment with different video formats to keep your content fresh (tutorials, vlogs, interviews, etc.).

5. Utilize YouTube Analytics:

- Use YouTube Analytics to understand when your audience is most active.
- Analyze the performance of your past videos to identify patterns and preferences.

6. Plan for Seasonal and Trendy Content:

- Incorporate seasonal or trending topics into your content calendar.
- Leverage popular events or trends to increase the discoverability of your videos.

7. Batch Production:

- Consider batching your video production. Record multiple videos in one sitting to save time.
- This allows you to stay ahead in your schedule and maintain Consistency.

8. Create Compelling Thumbnails and Titles:

- Thumbnails and titles are the first things viewers see. Make them eye-catching and relevant to increase click-through rates.

9. Optimize for SEO:

- Use relevant keywords in video titles, descriptions, and tags to improve searchability.
- Craft compelling video descriptions that provide additional context and encourage engagement.

10. Engage with Your Audience:

- Respond to comments and engage with your audience to build a community.
- Consider hosting live sessions or Q&A sessions to foster interaction.

11. Schedule in Advance:

- Utilize YouTube's scheduling feature to set a specific release time for your videos.
- This allows you to promote the release in advance and build anticipation.

12. Promote Across Platforms:

- Share teaser clips or announcements on other social media platforms to drive traffic to your YouTube channel.

13. Monitor and Adapt:

- Regularly review your analytics to identify what works and what doesn't.
- Adapt your strategy based on the feedback and performance of your videos.

14. Collaborate and Cross-Promote:

- Collaborate with other YouTubers to reach new audiences.
- Cross-promote each other's content to expand your reach.

15. Stay Updated on YouTube Policies:

- Be aware of YouTube's policies and guidelines to avoid any issues with your content.

16. Utilize YouTube Premiere:

- Consider using the Premiere feature for some of your videos. This allows you to build anticipation by creating a scheduled release with a countdown.

17. Create Playlists:

- Organize your videos into playlists to encourage viewers to watch more of your content. Playlists improve watch time and can boost your videos in YouTube's algorithm.

18. Monitor Trends and Algorithm Changes:

- Stay updated on YouTube trends and algorithm changes. Adapt your content strategy accordingly to take advantage of new features or trends.

19. Experiment with Publishing Times:

- Test different publishing times to find the optimal schedule for your audience. YouTube's analytics can help you identify peak activity periods.

20. Use Custom Thumbnails:

- Design custom thumbnails that are visually appealing and represent the content accurately. Thumbnails are critical for attracting clicks.

21. Encourage Subscriptions:

- Remind viewers to subscribe to your channel. Subscribers are more likely to see your new content and engage with it.

22. Create Compelling Intros:

- Capture viewers' attention with a compelling intro. The first few seconds are crucial for retaining viewers, so make them count.

23. Promote Evergreen Content:

- While trending topics are valuable, create evergreen content that remains relevant over time. This helps in maintaining a consistent flow of views.

24. Optimize Video End Screens and Cards:

- Use end screens and cards to promote other videos and playlists or encourage viewers to subscribe. This helps in keeping the audience engaged.

25. Host Giveaways or Contests:

- Increase engagement by hosting giveaways or contests. Encourage viewers to participate by liking, commenting, and sharing your videos.

26. Thoroughly Research Keywords:

- Invest time in researching and selecting the right keywords for your videos. This enhances the discoverability of your content.

27. Promote High-Performing Videos:

- Identify your top-performing videos and promote them on your or other marketing channels to capitalize on their success.

28. Invest in High-Quality Production:

- Aim for high production quality to make your videos visually appealing. This can contribute to better viewer retention and a positive impression of your brand.

29. Track Competitor Activity:

- Keep an eye on your competitors. Analyze their successful strategies and see if there are opportunities for you to differentiate or improve upon them.

30. Build a Brand Identity:

- Develop a consistent brand identity across your videos. This includes visuals, tone, and overall style, which helps create a memorable channel.

Remember, YouTube success is often a gradual process, so be patient and continually refine your strategy based on audience feedback and performance metrics.

Consistency and Frequency for Audience Engagement

Regarding audience engagement on YouTube, Consistency and regularity are two of the most important criteria. When developing a successful marketing plan for YouTube, it is necessary to establish a consistent schedule and maintain a continual stream of high-quality material. Here are some important things to keep in mind:

Communication and Branding that is consistent:

Create a distinct brand identity for your YouTube channel and ensure it is evident. A recognized logo, channel art, and consistent message are all things that fall under this category. This contributes to establishing a powerful brand presence, making it simpler for viewers to identify the material you provide.

Content Calendar: To organize the release of your videos, you need to create a content calendar. It is essential to maintain Consistency; therefore, make it a goal to submit films at regular intervals, whether once a day, once a week, or twice a week. Using this method helps to develop anticipation among the members of your audience.

Even though maintaining Consistency is essential, it is of equal significance to emphasize the quality of the information you produce. Focus on producing videos that are instructive, interesting, and engaging for the audience you are trying to reach.

Attend to the Needs of Your Audience:

Interacting with your audience and responding to comments left on your videos is important. This contributes to the development of a community that revolves around your channel and increases the extent to which your videos are seen on YouTube.

To achieve optimal timing, use analytics:

Determine the times of day when your audience is most engaged by analyzing the information provided by YouTube. During these peak hours, you should schedule the release of your videos to optimize both exposure and interaction.

Create a Variety of Content Types:

Make available a wide range of information to appeal to the many interests that are present within your target audience. Tutorials, product evaluations, videos from behind the scenes, and other types of content may fall under this category. You can maintain the appeal and relevance of your channel by diversifying the information you upload.

Advertising on Multiple Platforms:

You may reach a larger audience by uploading your films to YouTube and sharing them on other social media sites. You may increase the traffic that visits your YouTube channel by engaging in cross-promotion and stimulating fan interaction on other platforms.

Alerts and Subscriptions: To increase the number of viewers who subscribe to your channel, you should encourage them to enable alerts. They will be alerted anytime you release new material in this manner, increasing the probability of that content being immediately engaged.

Utilize YouTube tools: Use YouTube tools like end screens, annotations, and cards to guide viewers to additional videos on your channel that are pertinent to the topic at hand. This makes it easier to maintain visitors' attention for a longer period with your material.

Analyze and Adapt: Make it.

1. Make it a point to regularly analyze your YouTube statistics to understand what your audience finds most effective. Watch ti

2. e, click-through rate, and audience retention are all indicators that should be considered. Put this

Information to use to modify and improve your content strategy.

1. The title

Your videos' descriptions and tags should all be optimized with important keywords for search engine optimization. Because of this, your videos will be more likely to show in search results, and it will be simpler for the people you are trying to reach to find your material.

Construct Captivating Thumbnails:

The thumbnails you create should be captivating and appropriately depict your movie's content. To attract clicks, thumbnails are an essential component, and they have the potential to dramatically influence the performance of your movie.

Collaborate with Creators and Influencers: Work with other YouTubers or influencers in your field when collaborating with them. Your channel's exposure to a new audience and the acquisition of extra subscribers may both result from this. You should choose partners whose audience is similar to the demographic you are trying to reach.

Conduct competitions and Giveaways: To keep your audience interested, you should conduct competitions or giveaways. You should encourage viewers to like, comment on, and share your videos as a means of entry. The visibility of your material is increased as a result of this, in addition to the increased interaction it generates.

Make use of YouTube Analytics:

Review your YouTube Analytics regularly to acquire insights about the demographics of your viewers, the amount of time they watch, and common material. This information might serve as a guide for you as you work to improve your audience's engagement with your content strategy.

The incorporation of live streaming into your content strategy is highly recommended. YouTube often pushes live broadcasts to a wider audience, resulting in real-time interaction generated by live videos.

Playlists may be created by combining videos that are connected. Viewers are encouraged to watch many videos in a single sitting, increasing the total time spent watching and interacting on your channel.

Encourage evergreen content:

Produce material with a longer shelf life, sometimes called evergreen subject matter. This material continues to acquire views and interaction long after it was first made available to the public, demonstrating that it is still relevant.

Facilitate the Creation of User-Generated Material: Motivate your audience to generate and distribute material associated with your organization. Creating content by users not only fosters the development of communities but also functions as a kind of free promotion.

The strategic use of advertising:

Consider using advertisements on YouTube to increase your channel's popularity. You should direct your advertisements toward certain demographics, hobbies, or geographic places to reach your target audience.

Keep an eye on the trends and stay up to date:

Make sure you are up to date on the latest issues and trends that pertain to your expertise. Creating material that is both current and relevant has the potential to attract a greater number of users who are actively looking for the most recent information.

Optimize the duration of the Video: Pay attention to the duration of the video. The answer to this question is not universally applicable; nonetheless, gaining an insight into the preferences of your audience may assist you in determining the ideal duration for your films to maintain viewer engagement.

Create instructional material to provide your audience with something of worth and to provide them with benefits. Creating useful videos, tutorials, and how-to guides will help you position yourself as an expert in your preferred field.

Fostering a feeling of community among your audience is an important aspect of community engagement. It is important to keep your subscribers up to date. Thus, responding to comments, asking for input, and considering developing a community tab is important.

Through these extra tactics, you can further improve your marketing efforts on YouTube and construct a vibrant audience that is actively engaged with your channel.

CHAPTER 6: GROWING YOUR SUBSCRIBER BASE

Strategies for Increasing Subscribers Organically

Increasing subscribers organically on YouTube requires strategic planning, consistent effort, and high-quality content. Here are some effective strategies to help you grow your YouTube channel organically:

1. **Create High-Quality Content:**

· Focus on producing valuable, entertaining, and relevant content for your target audience.

· Invest in good video and audio quality to enhance the viewing experience.

· Be consistent with your content style and niche.

2. Optimize Video Titles and Thumbnails:

· Craft compelling and descriptive video titles that communicate the content of your videos.

· Design eye-catching thumbnails that accurately represent your video and encourage clicks.

3. Use Keywords Effectively:

· Research relevant keywords using tools like Google Keyword Planner or YouTube's search suggest feature.

· Incorporate these keywords naturally into your video titles, descriptions, and tags.

4. Engage with Your Audience:

· Respond to comments on your videos to build a sense of community.

· Ask questions in your videos to encourage viewer engagement.

· Consider hosting live streams or Q&A sessions to interact with your audience in real time.

5. Promote on Social Media:

· Share your videos on social media platforms to reach a broader audience.

· Utilize platforms like Instagram, Twitter, and Facebook to promote your YouTube content.

6. Collaborate with Other YouTubers:

· Partner with other content creators in your niche for collaborations.

· Cross-promote each other's channels to tap into each other's audience.

7. Create Playlists:

· Organize your videos into playlists to keep viewers on your channel longer.

· Playlists can help improve the overall watch time, a crucial factor in YouTube's algorithm.

8. Utilize End Screens and Cards:

· Add end screens to your videos to encourage viewers to watch more of your content.

· Use YouTube cards to link to other relevant videos or your channel.

9. Run Contests and Giveaways:

· Encourage viewers to subscribe by running contests or giveaways.

· Make subscribing a requirement for entry and promote the contest across your social media channels.

10. Optimize Channel Page:

· Ensure your channel banner, about section, and playlists are well-organized and visually appealing.

· communicate the value of your channel and why viewers should subscribe.

11. Analytical Insights:

· Use YouTube Analytics to understand what works well and adjust your content strategy accordingly.

· Pay attention to watch time, click-through rates, and audience demographics.

12. Create Compelling Channel Trailer:

· Craft an engaging channel trailer that introduces new visitors to your content.

· communicate the value proposition of your channel and why viewers should subscribe.

13. Encourage Subscriptions in Videos:

· Include verbal calls to action in your videos, encouraging viewers to subscribe.

· Place subscription reminders strategically throughout your video content.

14. Utilize YouTube Shorts:

· Create short, engaging videos specifically designed for YouTube Shorts.

· The Shorts feature can help your content reach a wider audience and attract new subscribers.

15. Optimize for Mobile Viewing:

· Many viewers watch YouTube on mobile devices, so ensure your content is mobile-friendly.

· Check the video formatting, readability, and overall smartphone user experience.

16. Leverage Trends and Seasonal Content:

· Stay updated on current trends and create content around popular topics.

· Create seasonal or timely content that aligns with holidays or events relevant to your niche.

17. Create Compelling Thumbnails:

· Thumbnails play a crucial role in attracting clicks. Design thumbnails that stand out and pique curiosity.

· Maintain Consistency in your thumbnail style to make your brand easily recognizable.

18. Use Playlists Strategically:

· Group related videos into playlists to encourage binge-watching.

· Create themed playlists that showcase your expertise in a specific area.

19. Monitor YouTube Analytics:

· Regularly analyze YouTube Analytics to understand viewer behavior and preferences.

· Identify patterns in successful videos and replicate those elements in future content.

20. Host Giveaways and Contests:

· Encourage viewers to participate in contests and giveaways with the condition of subscribing to your channel.

· Promote these events on social media platforms to attract a wider audience.

21. Participate in YouTube Communities:

· Engage with other creators and viewers in YouTube communities.

· Share your insights, collaborate with others, and contribute positively to the platform.

22. Create Evergreen Content:

· Develop content that remains relevant over time.

· Evergreen videos can continue to attract new subscribers long after their initial release.

23. Capitalize on End-of-Video Screen Elements:

· Utilize end screens to recommend additional videos and prompt viewers to subscribe.

· Direct viewers to playlists or your most recent upload to keep them engaged.

24. Stay Consistent:

· Consistency is key. Stick to a regular uploading schedule to keep your audience engaged.

· A consistent posting frequency helps build trust and expectations with your subscribers.

By combining these strategies and adapting them to your specific niche and audience, you can steadily increase your YouTube subscribers organically over time. Remember, building a successful channel is a marathon, not a sprint. Focus on creating valuable content and building genuine connections with your audience.

Collaborations and Cross-Promotions

Collaborations and cross-promotions on YouTube can be powerful strategies to expand your audience, increase engagement, and boost your channel's growth. Here are some tips to effectively leverage collaborations and cross-promotions on YouTube marketing:

1. Identify Suitable Partners:
- Look for YouTubers or channels with a similar target audience but not direct competitors.
- Consider creators with a complementary content style or niche.

2. Build Relationships:
- Engage with potential collaborators on social media.
- Attend industry events or join online communities to connect with creators.

3. Plan Joint Content:
- Create content that is beneficial for both audiences.
- Brainstorm ideas that showcase the strengths of both channels.

4. Align Branding:

- Ensure that the collaboration aligns with both channels' Branding and values.
- Consistent messaging helps maintain credibility.

5. Cross-Promote:

- Promote each other's videos within your content.
- Use cards, end screens, and verbal calls to action to encourage viewers to check out the partner's channel.

6. Leverage Community Tab:

- Utilize YouTube's community tab to share updates, behind-the-scenes, and promote collaborations.

7. Host Challenges or Contests:

- Engage audiences with challenges or contests that involve both channels.
- Encourage viewers to participate and cross-promote contest-related content.

8. Utilize Social Media:

- Share teaser trailers or behind-the-scenes footage on other social media platforms.
- Collaborate on social media campaigns to generate pre-release buzz.

9. Create Playlists:

- Feature each other's videos in curated playlists.
- Playlists encourage continuous viewing and improve search visibility.

10. Guest Appearances:

- Make guest appearances on each other's channels.
- This can include interviews, co-hosting, or participating in collaborative projects.

11. Promote Each Other's Merchandise:

- If applicable, cross-promote merchandise or products.
- Offer exclusive discounts or bundle deals for viewers of both channels.

12. Track and Analyze:

- Monitor the performance of collaborative content.
- Use YouTube Analytics to understand the impact on subscriber growth, watch time, and engagement.

13. Maintain Consistency:

- Consistency is key to long-term success.
- Plan future collaborations to keep the momentum going.

14. Communicate Effectively:

- Communicate expectations, timelines, and promotional efforts.
- Regular communication ensures a smooth collaboration process.

15. Be Open to Different Formats:

- Explore collaboration formats like joint live streams, split-screen videos, or multi-part series.

16. Create Exclusive Content:

- Offer exclusive content on one another's channels to incentivize viewers to subscribe to both channels.
- This could be behind-the-scenes footage, extended interviews, or special editions of your regular content.

17. Utilize YouTube Premieres:

- Coordinate with your collaborator to use YouTube Premieres for video releases.

- This can create a shared live viewing experience for both audiences.

18. Host Virtual Events:

- Organize virtual events like Q&A sessions, webinars, or workshops together.
- This allows both channels to engage with a broader audience simultaneously.

19. Joint Giveaways:

- Conduct joint giveaways to encourage audience participation.
- Include entry criteria that involve subscribing to both channels, leaving comments, and sharing the collaborative content.

20. Feature Each Other in Channel Trailers:

- Swap or feature each other in your channel trailers.
- This ensures that new visitors are immediately introduced to the collaborative effort.

21. Share Resources and Expertise:

- Collaborate on videos where each creator shares their expertise.
- This can introduce both channels to new audiences interested in diverse content.

22. Themed Collaborations:

- Plan collaborations around specific themes or trends relevant to both channels.
- This can capitalize on trending topics and increase the likelihood of reaching a wider audience.

23. Incorporate Interactive Elements:

- Integrate interactive elements like polls, quizzes, or challenges involving both channels' audiences.
- This boosts engagement and encourages cross-channel interaction.

24. Cross-Promote in Video Descriptions:
- Include links to each other's channels in video descriptions.
- Mention the collaboration and encourage viewers to check out the partner's content.

25. Share Analytics and Insights:
- Collaborate on analyzing data and share insights.
- Discuss what worked well, areas for improvement, and strategies for future collaborations.

26. Engage with Combined Audiences:
- Host joint live sessions where both creators actively engage with the combined audience.
- Respond to comments and questions, and create a sense of community.

27. Collaborate Across Platforms:
- Extend collaborations beyond YouTube to other platforms like Instagram, Twitter, or TikTok.
- This multi-platform approach can maximize reach.

28. Collaborative Playlists:
- Create shared playlists featuring each other's content.
- This can encourage viewers to explore more from both channels.

29. Diversify Collaborator Types:
- Collaborate with creators of different sizes, from micro-influencers to larger channels.

- This broadens your reach and introduces your content to varied audience segments.

30. Seek Sponsorships Together:

- Explore joint sponsorship opportunities.
- This can increase the revenue potential for both channels and enhance the collaborative experience.

Remember to adapt these strategies based on the nature of your content, audience preferences, and your collaboration goals. Building strong, mutually beneficial partnerships can significantly contribute to the success and growth of your YouTube channel.

Responding to Comments and Feedback

When it comes to developing a robust online community and enhancing your entire marketing plan, one of the most important aspects is responding to comments and criticism posted on your YouTube channel. Below are some suggestions that will help you reply to comments and criticism on YouTube in an efficient manner:

Always be on time: Give a prompt response to the comments that have been left. By doing so, you demonstrate to your audience that you are actively involved and that you respect their advice.

2. Express gratitude: To begin your answer, you should express gratitude to the audience for watching your video and leaving a remark. This feature facilitates the development of a good connection with your audience.

3. Make your responses more personal by addressing the person who commented by their name whenever feasible. A human touch is added to your comments when you personalize them, and viewers sense a stronger connection to your channel whenever you do so.

4. Maintain a pleasant Attitude: Even if the remark is critical, you should maintain a pleasant reply. The best way to address issues is with a positive and understanding attitude. Take care not to get defensive.

5. Address Concerns in a Professional Manner: If a viewer expresses concern or provides constructive criticism, you should

answer professionally and demonstrate that you value their comments. Make the most of this chance to improve and enrich the material you have created.

6. Inspire Participation: Inspire viewers to offer their views, opinions, and experiences by encouraging them to participate. You should ask open-ended questions to encourage more conversation in the comments area.

7. Take Care to Handle bad remarks. If you are given bad remarks, you should respond to them with compassion and a desire to comprehend the observer's viewpoint. Stay away from disputes and avoid being combative at all costs.

8. admit and Correct Errors: If you have made a mistake in your video or supplied information that is not correct, you should admit it and appreciate the viewer for bringing it to your attention. You should correct the error and clarify your commitment to providing accurate material.

To cultivate community among your audience, you should actively participate in discussions. This will lead to the promotion of a community vibe. Not only should you respond to comments aimed at you, but you should also communicate with viewers who are now conversing with one another.

10. Make wise use of humor: Humor can be an excellent way to connect with your audience; however, it is important to utilize it responsibly, particularly when responding to unfavorable remarks. Ensure that your sense of humor is not condescending and does not come off as dismissive.

11. Instruct viewers to access more content: You should connect viewers to another video if they ask a question that can be answered in another video or if you have information that is relevant to the inquiry. Increased interaction and continued viewership on your channel are both possible outcomes.

12. Recognize and Appreciate favorable remarks: It is important to make an effort to recognize and appreciate favorable remarks. Responding to positive comments helps establish a good attitude within your community and promotes additional positive involvement from members of the community.

Create a Commenting Policy, Number Thirteen: Establish unambiguous standards for the comment area of your website. Providing your audience with this information helps them establish expectations on the kind of remarks that are appropriate. Ensure that these regulations are routinely enforced to keep the online environment healthy.

14. Use Keywords and Tags in Your comments: Make sure to include key phrases and tags pertinent to your comments. Not only does this assist with search engine optimization, but it also has the potential to attract additional visitors looking for information comparable to what you have.

15. Provide Helpful answers: If a viewer brings up an issue or a difficulty, you should provide answers that others may use. By supporting your viewers, you demonstrate your dedication to them, regardless of whether the problem is a technical one with your video or a concern regarding the information you have created.

16. Modify Effectively: Be sure to watch your comment area and delete any remarks deemed unsuitable or spam as soon as possible. Doing so ensures that your viewers will have a pleasant and risk-free experience.

17. Highlight the Contributions of Some Viewers: If a viewer contributes helpful ideas, recommendations, or more information in the comments section, it is important to appreciate and promote their work. As a result, others are inspired to participate more actively in the future.

18. Investigate the Use of Video Answers: Consider the possibility of producing video answers to certain remarks or inquiries. This not only allows you to add a personal touch but also allows you to answer frequent questions or concerns raised by your audience.

19. Address Frequently Asked Questions If you see that the comments include questions that are asked often, you could either include a section labeled "Frequently Asked Questions" (FAQ) in the descriptions of your videos or think about producing a film that is just devoted to answering these prevalent concerns.

Twenty and a half: Encourage Notifications and Subscriptions: Remind viewers politely to subscribe to your channel and enable alerts so that they may stay up to speed with future developments. This facilitates building a subscriber base that is more committed and engaged.

21. Collaborate with Viewers: When it is acceptable, work with the people watching your content. Make sure they feel like they are actively participating in expanding your channel by soliciting their feedback on forthcoming material, including them in decision-making processes, and including them in the process.

22. Use Pinned Comments: Consider the possibility of pinning significant comments or answers at the top of the comment area. This makes it possible for anybody who visits your video to quickly see any important information, announcements, or explanations that may be there.

23. Demonstrate Authenticity: When responding, demonstrate that you are authentic. Viewers highly value sincerity, which contributes to developing trust and strengthens the relationship between you and your audience.

Remember that the most important thing is to cultivate a positive and participatory community around your content. Engaging with your audience consistently via comments may help you establish a devoted fan base and can substantially contribute to the effectiveness of your marketing efforts on YouTube.

Using Community Features to Foster Interaction

Fostering interaction on YouTube through community features is crucial for building a loyal audience and increasing the visibility of your content. Here are some strategies to leverage community features on YouTube for marketing purposes:

1. **Community Tab:**
   - **Regular Updates:** Use the Community Tab to share updates, behind-the-scenes content, and announcements. This keeps your audience engaged between video uploads.
   - **Polls:** Create polls to involve your audience in decision-making. This can include choosing video topics and content formats or deciding on merchandise designs.
1. **YouTube Live:**
   - **Live Q&A Sessions:** Host live Q&A sessions where viewers can ask questions in real-time. This creates a direct and immediate connection with your audience.
   - **Product Launches:** Use live streams to launch new products or services, allowing your audience to be part of the unveiling.
1. **Comments Section:**
   - **Engagement:** Respond to comments on your videos. Encourage discussions by asking questions in your

video and prompting viewers to share their thoughts in the comments.

- **Feature Top Comments:** Highlight top comments or questions in subsequent videos. This encourages viewers to engage in meaningful discussions.

1. **Contests and Giveaways:**

- **Encourage Participation:** Host contests or giveaways and ask viewers to participate by commenting, liking, or sharing the video. This increases engagement and helps in reaching a wider audience.

- **Announce Winners:** Make sure to announce winners through your videos, creating excitement and a sense of community.

1. **Custom Emojis and Badges:**

- **Channel Memberships:** If you have a YouTube channel with memberships enabled, create custom emojis and badges for your members. This provides a sense of exclusivity and recognition for loyal supporters.

- **Live Chat Recognition:** Use custom emojis and badges to recognize and appreciate members during live streams, fostering a sense of community.

1. **Collaborations and Shoutouts:**

- **Feature Community Contributions:** Give shoutouts to viewers who contribute valuable content, such as fan art or remixes. This encourages others to get involved.

- **Collaborate with Viewers:** Consider collaborating with your audience on special projects or featuring their content in your videos.

1. **Community Guidelines and Moderation:**

- **Set Clear Guidelines:** Establish community guidelines to maintain a positive and respectful environment.

- **Moderation:** Moderate comments and discussions to ensure a healthy and inclusive community.

1. **Analytics and Feedback:**

   - **Monitor Analytics:** Use YouTube analytics to understand the most effective community features. Adjust your strategy based on the data.

   - **Ask for Feedback:** Regularly ask your audience for feedback on the community features and content. This shows that you value their input.

By actively utilizing these community features, you can create a vibrant and engaged community around your YouTube channel, increasing brand loyalty and improving marketing outcomes.

CHAPTER 8: ANALYZING YOUTUBE ANALYTICS

Understanding Key Metrics and Performance Indicators

YouTube marketing involves creating and promoting content on the YouTube platform to reach and engage your target audience. To measure the success of your YouTube marketing efforts, it's important to monitor key metrics and performance indicators. Here are some key metrics to focus on:

1. **Views:**

   - **Total Views:** The total number of times your video has been watched. This metric gives you a general idea of your video's popularity.

   - **Unique Views:** The number of individual users who have watched your video at least once.

1. **Watch Time:**

   - **Total Watch Time:** The total number of minutes users have spent watching your videos. YouTube values watch time and can positively influence your video's visibility in search and recommendations.

1. **Subscribers:**

   - **Subscriber Growth:** The number of new subscribers gained over a specific period. A growing subscriber base indicates that your content is resonating with your audience.

1. **Click-Through Rate (CTR):**

   - **Thumbnail CTR:** The percentage of viewers who clicked on your video after seeing the thumbnail. A high CTR suggests that your thumbnail and title are compelling.

1. **Engagement:**
   - **Likes, Dislikes, Comments:** The number of likes, dislikes, and comments your videos receive. High engagement indicates that your content is sparking a reaction from viewers.

1. **Retention Rate:**
   - **Average View Duration:** The average time viewers spend watching your video. This metric helps identify where viewers may be dropping off.

1. **Conversion Metrics:**
   - **Clicks on Annotations/End Screens:** Measure how many viewers interact with the elements you've added to your video, such as annotations or end screens, which can drive traffic to other videos or external links.

1. **Traffic Sources:**
   - **YouTube Search, External, Suggested Videos:** Understand where your traffic comes from. This information helps you optimize your content for search or adjust your promotion strategy.

1. **Revenue and Monetization:**
   - **Ad Revenue:** If monetizing your content, track the revenue generated from ads on your videos.
   - **Affiliate Revenue:** If using affiliate marketing, track revenue generated from affiliate links in video descriptions.

1. **Demographics:**
   - **Age, Gender, Location:** Understand the demographics of your audience. This information can help you tailor your content to suit your target audience better.

1. **Playback Locations:**
   - **YouTube Watch Page, Embedded Players:** Identify where your videos are being watched. This insight can inform your content distribution strategy.

1. **Device Type:**
   - **Mobile, Desktop, Tablet:** Understand the devices your audience uses to watch your videos. Optimize your content for the most popular device types.

1. **Average Percentage Viewed:**
   - **Percentage of Video Viewed:** This metric shows the average percentage of a video that viewers watched. It helps you understand where viewers tend to drop off, allowing you to improve content to retain audience attention.

1. **Top Traffic Videos:**
   - **Identify which videos are driving the most traffic to your channel.** This information can guide your content strategy by helping you create more of what's working.

1. **Shoutouts and Collaborations:**
   - **Track the impact of collaborations or shoutouts from other YouTubers.** Monitor subscriber growth, views, and engagement around the time of such collaborations.

1. **Subscriber-to-View Conversion Rate:**
   - **Calculate the percentage of your subscribers who actually watch your videos.** A high conversion rate indicates a strong connection with your subscriber base.

1. **Social Shares:**

- **Measure how often your videos are shared on social media platforms.** This can extend your reach and attract new viewers.

1. **Community Tab Engagement:**

   - **If you can access the YouTube Community tab, track likes, comments, and shares.** This helps in building a community around your channel.

1. **Brand Lift Metrics:**

   - **Monitor brand lift metrics like ad recall and awareness if running YouTube ads.** This provides insights into the effectiveness of your advertising campaigns.

1. **Audience Retention Graph:**

   - **Analyze the audience retention graph for each video.** Identify points where viewers drop off and adjust your content strategy accordingly.

1. **Playlist Performance:**

   - **Evaluate the Performance of playlists on your channel.** Playlists can increase overall watch time and keep viewers engaged with your content.

1. **Channel Analytics - Overview:**

   - **Utilize the Channel Analytics Overview page for a holistic view of your channel's Performance.** This includes real-time views, estimated revenue, and top videos.

1. **Experimentation Metrics:**

   - **Monitor the results of any A/B testing or content experiments.** This could involve testing different thumbnails, titles, or video lengths to see what resonates best with your audience.

1. **Response to Call-to-Actions (CTAs):**

   - **Analyze how viewers respond to CTAs within your videos.** Track clicks on links, subscription buttons, or other interactive elements.

1. **Time of Upload and Scheduling:**

   - **Experiment with different upload times and schedules.** Use analytics to determine when your audience is most active and likely to watch your videos.

1. **Ad Engagement Metrics:**

   - **For ads on your videos, track metrics like view-through rate and engagement.** This provides insights into how viewers are interacting with ads.

Remember, YouTube analytics is a dynamic tool. Regularly review and adapt your strategy based on the data you collect. Combining these metrics will comprehensively understand your YouTube channel's Performance and audience engagement.

Adjusting Your Strategy Based on Analytics Insights

Adjusting your YouTube marketing strategy based on analytics insights is crucial for optimizing your efforts and achieving better results. Here are some key steps to help you make informed decisions:

1. **Regularly Monitor Analytics:**

   - Keep a close eye on YouTube Analytics to track key metrics such as views, watch time, engagement, click-through rate (CTR), and subscriber growth.

   - Identify trends over time to understand how your content performs and evolves.

1. **Audience Demographics:**
   - Analyze your audience's demographics, including age, gender, and location. This information can help you tailor your content to better resonate with your target audience.

1. **Top-performing Content:**
   - Identify your most successful videos regarding views, watch time, and engagement. Determine the common elements or topics that resonate well with your audience.
   - Consider creating more content similar to what has been successful in the past.

1. **Engagement Metrics:**
   - Pay attention to likes, comments, and shares. High engagement indicates that your audience finds the content interesting.
   - Respond to comments and engage with your audience to foster community.

1. **Click-Through Rate (CTR):**
   - Analyze the CTR of your thumbnails and titles. If a video has a high impression rate but a low CTR, consider updating your thumbnail and title to make them more compelling.

1. **Watch Time and Retention:**
   - Focus on videos with high watch time and retention rates. YouTube algorithm favors videos that keep viewers engaged for longer periods.
   - Identify when viewers drop off and analyze if there are patterns or common reasons for the drop-off.

1. **SEO Optimization:**

- Check the Performance of your videos in search results. Optimize video titles, descriptions, and tags based on keywords that are relevant to your content.
- Utilize YouTube trends and keywords to stay current with popular topics.

1. **Experiment with Different Formats:**
   - Test different video formats, styles, and lengths to see what resonates best with your audience.
   - Use YouTube's A/B testing feature to experiment with different thumbnails, titles, or descriptions.

1. **Collaborations and Cross-Promotion:**
   - Analyze the Performance of collaboration videos or cross-promotions with other creators. Assess whether these collaborations bring in new viewers and subscribers.

1. **Adapt to Algorithm Changes:**
   - Stay informed about YouTube algorithm changes and adjust your strategy accordingly. Understanding the algorithm's work can help you optimize your content for better visibility.

1. **Consistency and Schedule:**
   - Analyze the Performance of videos based on posting schedules. Consider experimenting with different posting times and days to find the optimal schedule for your audience.

1. **Use External Tools:**
   - Leverage external analytics tools if necessary. Some third-party tools can provide additional insights into your YouTube performance.

1. **Mobile View Analysis:**

- Examine the percentage of views coming from mobile devices. If a significant portion of your audience watches on mobile, ensure your content is optimized for smaller screens and quick engagement.

1. **Playlist Performance:**

   - Check the Performance of playlists. If certain playlists are gaining traction, consider creating more content that fits into those thematic playlists.

1. **Subscriber Growth Analysis:**

   - Monitor the rate of subscriber growth. Identify videos that contribute significantly to subscriber acquisition and create more content aligned with those themes.

1. **Geographical Insights:**

   - Utilize geographical data to understand where your audience is concentrated. Tailor your content or marketing efforts to cater to specific regions or time zones.

1. **Promote High-Performing Videos:**

   - Use high-performing videos to cross-promote other content. Add end screens and cards to encourage viewers to watch more of your videos.

1. **Experiment with Monetization:**

   - If you're eligible for monetization features, analyze how different monetization options (ads, memberships, merchandise) impact viewer engagement and revenue. Adjust your approach based on the results.

1. **Community Tab Engagement:**

- If you have access to the Community tab, monitor engagement on posts. Use this feature to interact with your audience, share updates, and gather feedback.

1. **Competitor Analysis:**

   - Analyze the Performance of competitors in your niche. Identify trends or content styles that resonate with their audience and consider adopting similar strategies.

1. **Referral Traffic Sources:**

   - Check where your traffic comes from outside of YouTube (e.g., social media, external websites). Focus on channels that drive significant traffic and optimize your presence on those platforms.

1. **Test Thumbnails and Titles:**

   - Conduct A/B testing for thumbnails and titles. Experiment with different visual elements and wording to see what attracts more clicks.

1. **Review Historical Data:**

   - Look at historical data to identify patterns or seasonal trends in your content's Performance. Adjust your content calendar to align with these trends.

1. **Evaluate Ad Performance:**

   - If you run YouTube ads, analyze the performance metrics. Optimize targeting, ad format, and creative elements based on what resonates best with your target audience.

1. **Accessibility and Closed Captions:**

   - Analyze the impact of closed captions on engagement. Ensure your videos are accessible by adding accurate captions, as this can improve watch time and searchability.

1. **Diversify Content Types:**

   - Introduce various content types such as tutorials, vlogs, Q&A sessions, or live streams. Analyze which formats generate more engagement and adapt your content strategy accordingly.

Remember to approach adjustments iteratively and be patient as you test and refine your strategies based on analytics insights. Regularly reassessing your approach will help you stay agile in the dynamic landscape of YouTube marketing.

Staying Relevant with Current YouTube Trends

Maintaining relevance with the most recent trends on YouTube is essential for successful marketing on YouTube. Maintaining a connection with your audience and being one step ahead of the competition is made easier by staying abreast of the most recent trends, which are always shifting on the platform. To ensure that you remain relevant with the latest trends on YouTube, here are some tips:

Regularly keep an eye on the trends on YouTube: By consistently checking the trending page on YouTube, examining prominent channels in your field, and following important hashtags on social media sites, you can ensure that you are up to date on the most recent trends. Your understanding of the material that resonates with the audience will be improved due to this.

Develop Content That Is Trending: After identifying the current trends, you should try to integrate them into your content strategy. However, be sure that the trends align with your brand and the audience you are trying to reach. Maintaining the integrity of your company requires you to provide content that is not just genuine but also on trend.

Attend to the Needs of Your Audience: Connecting with your audience via comments, likes, and shares may help create a feeling of community between you and them. Please respond to the comments left on your videos, solicit input from viewers, and encourage them to express their ideas. This kind of involvement helps you establish a devoted following and gives you valuable information about what intrigues your viewers.

Collaborate with Other YouTubers: Working with other YouTubers might help your channel reach new viewers and increase its popularity. Look for influential or creative people in your field, and then suggest ideas for cooperation that would benefit both of you. By doing so, you will be able to boost your channel's exposure and tap into the subscriber base maintained by each other.

Be sure to stay up to speed on the latest YouTube features. YouTube is always releasing new tools and features for content producers. Always ensure you are up to speed on these developments, and investigate how you may use them to improve your material. As an illustration, YouTube Shorts, live streaming, and community postings are all features that may assist you in diversifying the content you produce and engaging with your audience in various ways.

Prioritize the optimization of your video thumbnails and titles by paying close attention to each of these aspects. These are important considerations that play a role in determining whether or not people click on your video. Examine the titles and thumbnails of videos currently popular in your specialized field, and try out various styles to see which one is most effective for your audience.

Put Analytics to Work for You: Applications. Your YouTube channel's metrics should be analyzed regularly to determine which videos are doing well and why. It is important to recognize trends, such as the sort of material, keywords, or duration of the video that connects with your audience. Use this information to improve your content strategy and concentrate on developing material that is in line with your audience's tastes.

YouTube's algorithm is always being updated. Thus, it is important to adapt to these changes. Be sure to keep yourself updated on any modifications to the algorithm and adjust your approach appropriately. If you can get an understanding of how the algorithm ranks the material, you will be able to optimize your films for increased exposure.

You should use YouTube Shorts, a tool that enables you to produce short videos that are entertaining and presented in a vertical manner. Utilizing YouTube Shorts will assist you in reaching a larger audience and capitalizing on the trend of short films that are easily digestible. Short-form content is becoming more popular on platforms such as TikTok.

Incorporating influencer marketing involves locating influential people in your specialized field and working with them to address their audience. Your business may gain credibility and visibility via influencer marketing, particularly if the material associated with the influencer is congruent with your brand's ideals.

Investigate specialized Communities: Search for the specialized communities and forums associated with the information you provide. Participate in these groups, post your films, and ask for comments simultaneously. Your target audience's precise requirements and preferences might be better understood using this information.

Attempt Live Streaming: Live streaming is a strong method that allows you to engage with your audience in real-time. To maintain your audience's interest and foster community, you may consider doing live question-and-answer sessions, material behind the scenes, or interactive challenges.

Create Video That Is Educational YouTube continues to be a popular platform for educational videos. It is a good idea to think about producing instructional videos, how-to manuals, or educational material that the visitors will find valuable. Research and answer the concerns or difficulties most often asked within your area.

Maintain an active social presence by using the power of other social media channels to promote your work on YouTube. You may increase the traffic that visits your YouTube channel by sharing updates, behind-the-scenes films, or excerpts. Through the use of cross-promotion, you may reach a more extensive audience.

It is important to ensure that your video is suited for mobile viewing since many YouTube visitors access the social media platform from their mobile devices. When viewing videos on smaller displays, paying attention to the formatting, subtitles, and general visual attractiveness is important.

Take Part in Challenges and Trends: Monitoring successful challenges and trends within your specific specialization or across the platform is important. Encourage participation in these trends by producing innovative and relevant material. Your exposure will rise as a result, and you will be able to attract a larger audience.

Explore a Wide Range of Content kinds: Experiment with various content kinds, such as video blogs, interviews, or narratives. You can maintain the freshness of your channel and appeal to a larger variety of viewers by diversifying the material you upload.

Maintain a Close Eye on Your Rivals: Always be aware of your rivals' actions. Examine the videos that have made them successful, their interaction tactics, and overall content strategy. What works in your niche may be gleaned from this, which can give significant insights.

Invest in grade Production: Utilizing production qualities of a high grade may help your content stand out from the crowd. You should invest in high-quality equipment, video editing, and production quality in general. This can make the viewing experience more enjoyable for the audience and persuade them to continue to subscribe to your channel.

Maintain a flexible mindset and be open to receiving feedback: viewers' tastes and trends on YouTube may change on the go. Remain flexible and receptive to your audience's comments and suggestions. You should continuously monitor comments, run surveys, and utilize feedback to continuously improve your content strategy.

You can traverse the ever-changing world of YouTube trends and keep a strong presence in the platform community if you remain proactive, adaptable, and involved with your audience. Your plan should be reevaluated and modified regularly to accommodate your audience's and the platform's ever-changing tastes.

Participating in Challenges and Viral Content

Participating in challenges and creating viral content can be an effective strategy for YouTube marketing, as it helps increase engagement, reach a wider audience, and build a stronger connection with your viewers. Here are some tips to leverage challenges and viral content for your YouTube marketing efforts:

1. **Stay Relevant:**
   - Keep an eye on current trends and popular challenges within your niche.
   - Understand your target audience and create content that aligns with their interests.

1. **Create Unique Challenges:**
   - Put a unique spin on existing challenges or create your own to stand out.
   - Ensure your challenges are entertaining, shareable, and easy for viewers to participate in.
1. **Engage with Your Community:**
   - Encourage your viewers to participate by creating response videos or sharing their experiences.
   - Respond to comments and engage with your audience to foster community.
1. **Leverage Influencers and Collaborations:**
   - Collaborate with other YouTubers or influencers to amplify the reach of your challenge.
   - Cross-promotion can introduce your content to new audiences.
1. **Optimize Titles and Thumbnails:**
   - Craft compelling titles that generate curiosity and encourage clicks.
   - Design attention-grabbing thumbnails that clearly convey the content of your video.
1. **Use Social Media:**
   - Share teasers or highlights of your challenge on other social media platforms to generate interest.
   - Utilize relevant hashtags to increase discoverability.
1. **Timing is Key:**
   - Release your challenge or viral content strategically when your audience is most active.
   - Consider piggybacking on existing trends or events for added visibility.

1. **Quality Production:**
   - Ensure your video is well-produced and visually appealing.
   - Invest time in editing, sound quality, and overall presentation to enhance viewer experience.

1. **Encourage Sharing:**
   - Include calls to action in your video, asking viewers to like, share, and subscribe.
   - Make it easy for viewers to share their participation in your challenge on social media.

1. **Track Analytics:**
   - Monitor the Performance of your challenge or viral content using YouTube analytics.
   - Understand what worked well and use those insights to refine your future strategies.

1. **Create a Series:**
   - Turn your challenge into a series to keep viewers engaged over multiple episodes.
   - Tease upcoming challenges to build anticipation and encourage subscribers to return.

1. **Encourage User-Generated Content:**
   - Motivate your audience to create their own content related to your challenge.
   - Feature user-generated content in your videos to showcase community involvement.

1. **Behind-the-Scenes Content:**
   - Provide behind-the-scenes footage of the making of your challenge.

- Share bloopers or funny moments to add a personal touch and humanize your brand.

1. **Utilize YouTube Shorts:**

   - Leverage YouTube Shorts to create concise and engaging content that may be more shareable.
   - Shorts can also be a great format for challenges due to their brief nature.

1. **Incorporate Trends Responsibly:**

   - Stay informed about broader cultural and internet trends.
   - Be mindful of the context and potential controversies when participating in challenges.

1. **Themed Challenges:**

   - Align your challenges with specific themes or events (seasonal, holidays, etc.).
   - Themed challenges can resonate well with viewers and capitalize on timely interests.

1. **Interactive Elements:**

   - Introduce interactive elements such as polls, quizzes, or challenges that viewers can participate in while watching.
   - Engaging viewers actively can enhance their experience and increase retention.

1. **Optimize for Mobile Viewing:**

   - Many viewers access YouTube on mobile devices, so ensure your content is optimized for small screens.
   - Use text overlays or subtitles to convey key information, especially in short-form content.

1. **Collaborate with Your Audience:**

- Feature shoutouts or highlights from participants in your challenge.
- This fosters a sense of community and encourages more viewers to take part.

1. **Learn from Analytics:**
   - Analyze the metrics from your challenges to understand audience demographics, watch time, and engagement.
   - Use this data to refine your content strategy and tailor future challenges to your audience's preferences.

1. **Promote a Cause:**
   - Attach your challenge to a charitable cause or social issue.
   - This can enhance the impact of your content and demonstrate a commitment to social responsibility.

1. **Experiment with Content Formats:**
   - Try different content formats, such as vlogs, tutorials, or reaction videos, to present challenges in diverse ways.
   - Experimenting keeps your content fresh and appeals to a broader audience.

CHAPTER 10: MONETIZATION STRATEGIES

Exploring Ad Revenue Opportunities

Exploring ad revenue opportunities on YouTube involves understanding the platform's monetization features and implementing effective strategies to maximize your earnings. Here are several key aspects to consider:

1. **Enable Monetization:**

   - To earn ad revenue on YouTube, you must join the YouTube Partner Program (YPP). Ensure your channel meets the eligibility requirements, such as having at least 1,000 subscribers and 4,000 valid public watch hours in the last 12 months.

1. **Create Quality Content:**

   - High-quality, engaging content attracts more viewers, leading to higher ad revenue. Understand your target audience and create content that resonates with them.

1. **Optimize Videos for Ads:**

   - Place ads strategically within your videos. Mid-roll ads appear during longer videos and can be more lucrative than pre-roll ads. However, be mindful not to interrupt the viewer's experience excessively.

1. **Diversify Content Types:**

   - Create a variety of content types to appeal to a broader audience. This can include tutorials, reviews, vlogs, and more. Diversifying your content helps attract different viewer demographics and increases your ad revenue potential.

1. **SEO Optimization:**

   - Use relevant keywords, tags, and descriptions to optimize your videos for search engines. This increases the likelihood of your videos appearing in search results, attracting more viewers and potential ad revenue.

1. **Build a Consistent Upload Schedule:**
   - Consistency is key on YouTube. Establish a regular upload schedule to keep your audience engaged and returning for more content. A dedicated audience contributes to higher ad revenue.

1. **Engage with Your Audience:**
   - Respond to comments, ask for feedback, and encourage viewers to subscribe and share your content. A highly engaged audience is more likely to watch your videos in their entirety, increasing ad revenue.

1. **Explore Sponsorships and Brand Deals:**
   - Collaborate with brands and sponsors to create sponsored content. This can provide an additional revenue stream beyond YouTube ads.

1. **Utilize YouTube Merchandise Shelf:**
   - If you have merchandise related to your channel, use the Merchandise Shelf feature to sell products directly from your videos. This can be an additional source of income.

1. **Join YouTube Memberships:**
   - If eligible, consider enabling channel memberships. Viewers can become channel members for a monthly fee, gaining access to exclusive perks. This can supplement your ad revenue.

1. **Stay Informed About YouTube Policies:**
   - Regularly check and adhere to YouTube's policies and guidelines to avoid issues impacting your ability to monetize your content.

1. **Utilize YouTube Shorts:**

- Leverage YouTube Shorts, a short-form video feature, to reach a wider audience. While Shorts don't directly monetize through ads, they can drive traffic to your main content, increasing overall ad revenue.

1. **Collaborate with Other YouTubers:**
   - Collaborations can expose your channel to new audiences. Partner with YouTubers in your niche to cross-promote each other's content and potentially gain more subscribers and views.

1. **Cross-Promote on Social Media:**
   - Share your YouTube videos on other social media platforms to expand your reach. Engage with your audience on various channels and direct them to your YouTube content.

1. **Experiment with Ad Formats:**
   - YouTube offers various ad formats, including skippable and non-skippable ads. Experiment with different formats to see which works best for your audience and generates higher revenue.

1. **Create Compelling Thumbnails and Titles:**
   - Thumbnails and titles are crucial for attracting clicks. Design eye-catching thumbnails and craft compelling titles that entice viewers to watch your videos, increasing your ad revenue potential.

1. **Utilize End Screens and Cards:**
   - Encourage viewers to watch more of your content by using end screens and cards. Link to relevant videos, playlists, or subscribe buttons to keep viewers engaged and increase your watch time.

1. **Optimize for Mobile Viewers:**

- A significant portion of YouTube's traffic comes from mobile devices. Ensure your videos are optimized for mobile viewing to cater to this audience, potentially increasing ad revenue.

1. **Participate in YouTube Premium Revenue:**

   - YouTube Premium subscribers pay a monthly fee for an ad-free experience. As a YouTube Partner, you can earn a share of the revenue generated from YouTube Premium subscribers watching your content.

1. **Monitor Analytics and Adjust Strategy:**

   - Regularly review YouTube Analytics to understand audience behavior, demographics, and performance metrics. Use this data to refine your content strategy and maximize ad revenue.

1. **Host Live Streams:**

   - Live streams provide an opportunity for real-time engagement with your audience. Viewers can send Super Chats, which are highlighted messages, for a fee. This can be an additional source of revenue during live broadcasts.

1. **Optimize for CTR (Click-Through Rate):**

   - Increase your video's click-through rate by creating compelling thumbnails and titles. A higher CTR can positively impact your video's Performance and ad revenue.

1. **Stay Advertiser-Friendly:**

   - Advertisers prefer brand-safe content. Avoid controversial or inappropriate topics to maintain a positive relationship with advertisers, leading to higher-quality ads and better revenue opportunities.

By combining these strategies and consistently producing high-quality, engaging content, you can build a successful YouTube channel with multiple revenue streams. Adapt your approach based on audience feedback and industry trends to stay relevant and maximize ad revenue opportunities.

Partnering with Brands and Sponsored Content

Partnering with brands and incorporating sponsored content into your YouTube marketing strategy can be a lucrative way to monetize your channel and build relationships within your niche. Here are some steps to guide you through the process:

1. **Build a Strong Channel:**
   - Before approaching brands, ensure your YouTube channel has a strong and engaged audience. Consistently create high-quality content that aligns with your niche and appeals to your target demographic.

1. **Identify Your Niche and Target Brands:**
   - Define your niche and target audience. This will help you identify brands that align with your content and have products or services relevant to your viewers.

1. **Create a Media Kit:**
   - Develop a media kit highlighting key information about your channel, such as demographics, audience size, engagement rates, and any notable achievements or milestones. Include your contact information and social media profiles.

1. **Reach Out to Brands:**

- Research potential brands that fit well with your content and audience. Contact them through email, social media, or their official website. Clearly communicate your value proposition and how a partnership can benefit both parties.

1. **Proposal and Rates:**
   - When approaching brands, be prepared to present a proposal outlining the collaboration details. Clearly state what you can offer, such as sponsored videos, product reviews, or integrated mentions. Include your rates and any specific terms or conditions.

1. **Disclose Sponsored Content:**
   - Be transparent with your audience by disclosing any sponsored content. This builds trust with your viewers and helps maintain authenticity.

1. **Negotiate Terms:**
   - Be open to negotiation. Discuss deliverables, timelines, exclusivity, and compensation. Ensure that both parties understand expectations and terms before finalizing any agreement.

1. **Create Compelling Sponsored Content:**
   - Once a partnership is established, create content that seamlessly integrates the brand's message into your style. Ensure it provides value to your audience and doesn't appear overly promotional.

1. **Promote Your Partners:**
   - Actively promote the brands you collaborate with across your social media channels. This demonstrates your commitment to the partnership and helps increase the overall reach of the sponsored content.

1. **Measure and Report Results:**
   - Provide the brands with analytics and insights on the Performance of the sponsored content. This includes views, engagement, click-through rates, and other relevant metrics. This information can be crucial for future collaborations.

1. **Maintain Authenticity:**
   - Only collaborate with brands that align with your personal brand and values. Authenticity is crucial for maintaining trust with your audience. If a product or service doesn't resonate with your content, declining the collaboration is better.

1. **Understand FTC Guidelines:**
   - Familiarize yourself with the Federal Trade Commission (FTC) guidelines regarding sponsored content and disclosures. Make sure to clearly disclose any paid partnerships to your audience in compliance with these regulations.

1. **Offer Different Collaboration Options:**
   - Provide brands with various collaboration options, such as sponsored videos, product placements, shoutouts, or exclusive discount codes. This flexibility can accommodate different brands' marketing goals and budgets.

1. **Build Relationships with PR Agencies:**
   - Connect with public relations (PR) agencies that represent multiple brands. Establishing relationships with these agencies can lead to steady collaboration opportunities and simplify the negotiation process.

1. **Invest in Professionalism:**

- Present yourself professionally in all communications with brands. Respond promptly to emails, maintain clear and concise communication, and deliver timely content. Professionalism enhances your credibility and makes brands more likely to work with you.

1. **Diversify Income Streams:**

   - While sponsored content can be a significant source of revenue, consider diversifying your income streams. Explore options like affiliate marketing, merchandise sales, channel memberships, and crowdfunding to create a more stable financial foundation.

1. **Track Metrics and Analytics:**

   - Use YouTube Analytics and other tracking tools to monitor the Performance of your sponsored content. Track metrics such as watch time, engagement, and conversion rates. This data is valuable for both you and the brands you collaborate with.

1. **Create a Win-Win Scenario:**

   - Aim to create partnerships that benefit both you and the brand. Understand the brand's goals and tailor your content to meet their objectives while ensuring your audience gains value from the collaboration.

1. **Be Selective with Partnerships:**

   - Quality is more important than quantity. Choose partnerships selectively, focusing on brands that genuinely resonate with your audience. A few well-curated collaborations are more impactful than numerous unrelated ones.

1. **Stay Updated on Industry Trends:**

   - Keep yourself informed about trends in your industry and the broader digital marketing landscape.

Awareness of current trends can help you position your content and collaborations to be more appealing to brands.

1. **Seek Long-Term Relationships:**
   - While one-off collaborations can be beneficial, building long-term relationships with brands can lead to more consistent and sustainable income. Establishing a positive track record with a brand may open doors for future opportunities.

By incorporating these tips into your approach, you can maximize the effectiveness of brand partnerships and sponsored content on your YouTube channel. Adapt your strategy based on the evolving digital marketing landscape and your audience's and potential collaborators' specific needs.

CHAPTER 11: YOUTUBE ADVERTISING

Overview of YouTube Ads and Formats

YouTube offers a variety of advertising options for businesses and marketers to promote their products and services. These ads can be displayed on desktop and mobile devices, reaching a massive audience. Here's an overview of YouTube ads and formats:

1. **TrueView Ads:**

   · **In-Stream Ads:** These are skippable video ads that play before, during, or after other YouTube videos. Advertisers only pay when viewers watch 30 seconds of the ad or the entire duration if it's shorter than 30 seconds.

·   **Non-Skippable Ads:** These are shorter video ads that viewers can't skip. Advertisers are charged based on impressions or clicks.

2. **Discovery Ads:**

· These ads appear on the YouTube homepage, search results, and alongside related videos. They consist of a thumbnail image and text and are charged when viewers click to watch the video.

3. **Bumper Ads:**

· These short, non-skippable ads are up to six seconds long. They are designed to quickly convey a message and are usually used for brand awareness.

4. **Masthead Ads:**

· These premium ads appear at the top of the YouTube homepage for desktop users and the mobile app home feed. They are typically sold on a cost-per-thousand-impressions (CPM) basis.

5. **Overlay Ads:**

· These are semi-transparent overlay ads that appear on the lower portion of a video. They can include text and images and are clickable.

6. **Display Ads:**

· traditional display ads appear next to the video suggestions list. They can be image or text ads and are typically charged on a cost-per-click (CPC) basis.

7. **YouTube Shopping Ads:**

· These ads allow advertisers to showcase their products on YouTube. They include a carousel of product images and information.

8. **Sponsored Cards:**

· These are small, clickable cards that appear within a video. They can display product information, related videos, or playlists.

9. **Video Discovery Ads:**

· These ads appear in YouTube search results, on the YouTube homepage, and as related videos on the right-hand side. Advertisers are charged when viewers click to watch the video.

10. **Live Stream Ads:**

· These ads appear on live streams on YouTube. They can be displayed before, during, or after the livestream.

11. **YouTube Ad Targeting:**

· YouTube offers various targeting options, allowing advertisers to reach specific demographics, interests, and behaviors. Targeting parameters include age, gender, location, interests, and keywords. This precision helps ensure that ads are shown to the most relevant audience.

12. **Ad Sequencing:**

· Advertisers can create a sequence of ads to tell a cohesive story or provide additional information. This involves showing a series of ads to viewers in a specific order, optimizing the messaging and engagement over multiple interactions.

13. **YouTube Analytics:**

· YouTube provides robust analytics tools to track the Performance of ads. Advertisers can analyze metrics such as views, click-through rates (CTR), conversion tracking, and audience demographics. These insights help refine strategies and improve the effectiveness of future campaigns.

14. **YouTube Ad Customization:**

· Advertisers can customize their ads to align with their brand identity. This includes adding interactive cards, end screens with call-to-action buttons, and branding watermarks to enhance the user experience.

15. YouTube Ad Formats for Mobile:

· Given the prevalence of mobile usage, YouTube offers ad formats optimized for mobile devices. This includes mobile-optimized end screens, ad formats suitable for vertical videos, and responsive display ads that adjust to different screen sizes.

16. YouTube for Action:

· YouTube for Action is a set of ad formats designed to drive actions, such as website visits, sign-ups, or purchases. These include TrueView for Action ads, which feature prominent calls-to-action and headline text overlays to encourage viewer engagement.

17. YouTube Ad Extensions:

· Similar to other online advertising platforms, YouTube allows ad extensions to provide additional information and encourage interaction. This can include location extensions, site link extensions, and callout extensions.

18. YouTube Ad Policies:

· Advertisers must adhere to YouTube's ad policies, which outline content guidelines, prohibited practices, and community standards. Understanding and following these policies ensures ads are approved and a positive brand image is maintained.

19. YouTube Ad Placement:

· Advertisers can choose specific ad placements, such as targeting channels, videos, or categories. Additionally, they can use contextual targeting to display ads on videos that match certain keywords or topics.

20. **YouTube Brand Lift Studies:**

· YouTube offers Brand Lift Studies to measure the impact of video ads on brand perception and awareness. These studies use surveys to assess key metrics and help advertisers understand the effectiveness of their campaigns.

YouTube's advertising platform continues to evolve, and staying informed about new features, updates, and best practices is essential for creating successful YouTube marketing campaigns.

Creating Effective Ad Campaigns for Your Brand

Creating effective ad campaigns on YouTube requires a strategic approach that aligns with your brand goals and targets your intended audience. Here's a step-by-step guide to help you create successful YouTube marketing campaigns:

1. Define Your Goals:

Clearly outline your objectives for the campaign. Understanding your goals will guide your overall strategy, whether it's increasing brand awareness, driving website traffic, or boosting product sales.

2. Identify Your Target Audience:

Define your target audience based on demographics, interests, and online behavior. This information will help you create content that resonates with your audience and positions your brand effectively.

3. Craft Compelling Content:

Create engaging and high-quality video content. Consider the following:

- **Hook Within First 5 Seconds:** Capture viewers' attention immediately.
- **Clear Message:** Communicate your brand message clearly and concisely.
- **Visual Appeal:** Ensure visually appealing videos with good production quality.
- **Mobile Optimization:** Many users watch YouTube on mobile, so optimize for smaller screens.

4. Utilize YouTube Ad Formats:

YouTube offers various ad formats to suit different goals:

- **TrueView In-Stream Ads:** Skippable ads that play before, during, or after videos.
- **TrueView Discovery Ads:** Promoted videos that appear in search results or as suggested videos.
- **Bumper Ads:** Short, non-skippable ads (6 seconds or less) to quickly convey your message.
- **Overlay Ads:** These are displayed as banner ads on the lower part of the video.

5. Implement Targeting Options:

Utilize YouTube's targeting options to reach your intended audience:

- **Demographic Targeting:** Age, gender, location, etc.
- **Interest Targeting:** Target users who are interested in specific topics.
- **Behavioral Targeting:** Reach users based on their online behavior.

6. Optimize for Keywords:

Use relevant keywords in your video titles, descriptions, and tags. This helps your videos appear in search results and increases discoverability.

7. Create a Compelling Thumbnail:

Design an eye-catching thumbnail that encourages users to click on your video. Ensure it reflects the content and sparks curiosity.

8. Implement Call-to-Action (CTA):

Include a clear and compelling call-to-action in your video, guiding viewers on the next steps you want them to take, such as visiting your website, subscribing, or making a purchase.

9. Monitor and Analyze Performance:

Regularly review analytics to understand how your ads are performing. Use this data to optimize your campaigns, focusing on what works best for your audience.

10. Test and Iterate:

Experiment with different ad creatives, targeting options, and ad formats. Regularly test and iterate based on the insights gained to improve campaign effectiveness.

11. Budgeting and Scheduling:

Set a realistic budget for your campaign and schedule ads at times when your target audience is most active.

12. Advertise Consistently:

Consistency is key to building brand awareness. Plan your campaigns to be ongoing and align them with your broader marketing strategy.

CHAPTER 12: CROSS-PROMOTION ON OTHER PLATFORMS

Integrating YouTube Marketing with Social Media

Integrating YouTube marketing with social media is a powerful strategy to enhance your online presence, engage with your audience, and drive traffic to your YouTube channel. Here are some effective ways to integrate YouTube marketing with social media:

1. **Create Cross-Platform Content:**
   - Develop content that can be shared across multiple platforms. For example, create teaser videos or highlights from your YouTube content to share on platforms like Instagram, Twitter, Facebook, and LinkedIn.

1. **Custom Thumbnails and Snippets:**
   - Design custom thumbnails for your YouTube videos that are visually appealing and shareable. Use snippets or highlights from your videos as teaser content on platforms like Instagram stories or Twitter.

1. **Leverage YouTube Cards and End Screens:**
   - Utilize YouTube's features like cards and end screens to link to your social media profiles. Direct viewers to follow you on various platforms for updates and additional content.

1. **Embed Videos on Social Media Platforms:**

- Share your YouTube videos directly on social media platforms by embedding them in your posts. This allows your audience to watch the content without leaving the social media environment.

1. **Live Streaming:**
   - Consider using live streaming features on both YouTube and social media platforms simultaneously. This can create a sense of urgency and exclusivity, encouraging users to follow you on multiple channels.

1. **Engage with Your Audience:**
   - Actively respond to comments on both YouTube and social media. Encourage your audience to share their thoughts, questions, and experiences related to your content. This engagement can increase visibility on both platforms.

1. **Run Contests and Giveaways:**
   - Host contests or giveaways that require participants to engage with your content on both YouTube and social media platforms. This can increase your reach and drive more traffic to your channel.

1. **Utilize Hashtags:**
   - Implement relevant hashtags in your YouTube video descriptions and promote them on social media. This can help increase discoverability and engage users in searching for content related to those hashtags.

1. **Collaborate with Influencers:**
   - Partner with influencers in your niche to create collaborative content. Share this content on both YouTube and social media to leverage each other's audiences and increase exposure.

1. **Promote Behind-the-Scenes Content:**
   - Share behind-the-scenes glimpses of your video creation process or day-to-day activities on social media. This can humanize your brand and build a stronger connection with your audience.

1. **Cross-Promote Playlists:**
   - Create playlists on YouTube and share them on social media. Playlists are a great way to organize content around specific themes, and cross-promoting them can encourage viewers to explore more of your videos.

1. **Create Social Media Teasers:**
   - Develop short teaser videos specifically for social media. These snippets should be intriguing enough to encourage viewers to click on your YouTube channel for the full content.

1. **Share Milestones and Achievements:**
   - Celebrate your YouTube milestones on social media, such as reaching a certain number of subscribers or views. This highlights your achievements and encourages social media followers to check out your YouTube channel.

1. **Promote Live Q&A Sessions:**
   - Host live Q&A sessions on YouTube and promote them on social media. Encourage your audience to submit questions in advance through social media platforms, creating anticipation for the live event.

1. **Utilize Instagram and Facebook Stories:**
   - Leverage the "swipe-up" feature on Instagram Stories if you can direct followers to your latest YouTube video. On platforms like Facebook, use stories to

provide updates and direct users to your YouTube content.

1. **Share User-Generated Content:**

   - Encourage your audience to create and share content related to your YouTube videos. Share and showcase this user-generated content on your social media channels, fostering a sense of community around your brand.

1. **Social Media Ad Campaigns:**

   - Run targeted ad campaigns on social media platforms to promote your YouTube channel or specific videos. Utilize platforms like Facebook Ads and Instagram Ads to reach a broader audience.

1. **Cross-Promote with Other YouTubers:**

   - Collaborate with other YouTubers in your niche and cross-promote each other's content on both YouTube and social media. This can introduce your channel to new audiences and strengthen your network within the community.

1. **Host Social Media Challenges:**

   - Create challenges related to your YouTube content and encourage your social media followers to participate. Ask them to share their challenge entries and experiences, creating a buzz around your content.

1. **Promote Exclusive Content:**

   - Offer exclusive content or behind-the-scenes footage to your social media followers as a reward for following your YouTube channel. This can incentivize cross-platform engagement.

1. **Optimize Social Media Profiles:**

- Ensure that your social media profiles prominently feature links to your YouTube channel. Use compelling descriptions and visuals to entice visitors to explore your videos.

1. **Share Playlists on Social Media:**
   - Share your YouTube playlists directly on social media. This allows users to binge-watch related content and increases the likelihood of subscribing to your channel.

1. **Host Polls and Surveys:**
   - Engage your audience by hosting polls and surveys on social media. Use the feedback to tailor your YouTube content based on the preferences and interests of your audience.

By combining these strategies, you can create a cohesive and effective marketing strategy that leverages both YouTube and social media platforms to grow your audience and increase engagement.

Expanding Your Reach Beyond YouTube

Expanding your reach beyond YouTube involves leveraging various strategies and platforms to enhance your YouTube marketing efforts. Here are some tips to help you broaden your reach:

1. **Social Media Integration:**

· Share your YouTube videos across all major social media platforms such as Facebook, Twitter, Instagram, and LinkedIn.

· Create engaging snippets or teasers to grab your audience's attention and encourage them to click through to your YouTube channel.

2. **Collaborate with Influencers:**

· Partner with influencers or content creators in your niche to reach their audience. This can introduce your channel to new viewers interested in your content.

3. **Cross-Promotion:**

· Collaborate with other YouTubers for cross-promotion. Mention each other in videos, create joint projects, or shout each other out. This can expose your content to new audiences.

4. **Email Marketing:**

· Build an email list and send regular updates to your subscribers about new videos or exclusive content. This direct communication can keep your audience engaged and aware of your latest uploads.

5. **Optimize Video Titles and Thumbnails:**

· Craft compelling video titles and design eye-catching thumbnails. This can increase click-through rates and improve the chances of your videos being recommended to a wider audience on YouTube.

6. **SEO Optimization:**

· Optimize video descriptions, tags, and closed captions for search engines. This will help your videos rank higher in YouTube searches and attract more organic traffic.

7. **Engage with Your Community:**

· Respond to comments on your videos and engage with your audience on social media. Building a community around your channel can promote word-of-mouth and increase visibility.

8. **Create Playlists:**

· Organize your videos into playlists. Playlists are more likely to appear in search results and can keep viewers on your channel longer, increasing your chances of being recommended to a broader audience.

9. **Utilize YouTube Ads:**

·Consider using YouTube Ads to target specific demographics. Paid promotions can help you reach a wider audience beyond your organic reach.

10. **Repurpose Content:**

·Repurpose your YouTube content into different formats (e.g., blog posts, podcasts, infographics) and share them on various platforms to reach audiences with different preferences.

11. **Host Contests and Giveaways:**

·Encourage engagement and attract new subscribers by hosting contests or giveaways. Ask participants to share your videos or subscribe to your channel to win.

12. **Attend and Sponsor Events:**

·Attend industry events or sponsor relevant conferences. Networking at such events can help you connect with potential collaborators, and sponsoring events can increase brand visibility.

13. **Podcasting:**

·Repurpose your YouTube content into podcast episodes. This allows you to reach audiences who prefer consuming content through audio platforms.

14. **Guest Appearances:**

·Guest appear on podcasts or YouTube channels within your niche. This can introduce you to new audiences and establish you as an authority in your field.

15. **Create a Website or Blog:**

· Establishing a website or blog allows you to showcase your YouTube content in a different format. It also helps with SEO and provides another avenue for audience engagement.

16. Utilize Forums and Communities:

· Participate in online forums and communities related to your niche. Share your expertise and subtly promote your YouTube channel when relevant.

17. Live Streaming on Other Platforms:

· Experiment with live streaming on Twitch, Facebook Live, or Instagram. Live content can attract a different audience and generate excitement around your brand.

18. Create Shareable Content:

· Craft content that is shareable and resonates with your audience. Encourage your viewers to share your videos on their social media, helping to increase your content's reach.

19. Translate and Subtitle Videos:

· Expand your international reach by providing subtitles in different languages. This makes your content accessible to a global audience, increasing the likelihood of reaching viewers from diverse regions.

20. Utilize Pinterest and TikTok:

· Create visually appealing pins for Pinterest linking to your YouTube videos. Additionally, explore short-form content on platforms like TikTok to showcase highlights and drive traffic to your main channel.

21. Offer Exclusive Content:

· Provide exclusive content to your audience through platforms like Patreon or a members-only section on your website. This can incentivize viewers to support your channel and access unique material.

22. Create a Newsletter:

· Start a newsletter to inform your audience about your latest content, upcoming projects, and behind-the-scenes insights. This direct communication can help build a stronger connection with your audience.

23. Engage in Trending Topics:

· Keep an eye on trending topics and create content that aligns with them. This can attract attention from viewers interested in popular discussions.

24. Monitor Analytics:

· Regularly analyze your YouTube analytics to understand your audience's demographics and preferences. Use this data to tailor your content and outreach strategies to suit your target audience better.

25. Build Partnerships with Brands:

· Collaborate with brands or businesses related to your niche. This can introduce your channel to their customer base and provide opportunities for co-promotion.

Remember, the key is to diversify your approach and adapt to trends and audience behavior changes. Combining multiple strategies and staying engaged with your audience can effectively expand your reach beyond YouTube.

CHAPTER 13: CASE STUDIES OF SUCCESSFUL YOUTUBE MARKETING

Examining Real-Life Examples of Brands and Individuals

YouTube marketing is a powerful strategy employed by both brands and individuals to reach and engage with their target audience. Here are a few real-life examples that illustrate successful YouTube marketing efforts:

1. **GoPro:**

    - **Approach:** GoPro, a brand known for its action cameras, has leveraged user-generated content effectively. They encourage their customers to share videos captured with GoPro cameras, showcasing extreme sports, travel, and adventure.

    - **Impact:** This strategy promotes their products and creates a community around the brand. The authenticity of user-generated content resonates with viewers and reinforces the brand's image.

1. **Dollar Shave Club:**

    - **Approach:** Dollar Shave Club disrupted the shaving industry with a humorous and viral YouTube video. The founder, Michael Dubin, starred in a low-budget video introducing the brand's subscription service with a witty script.

    - **Impact:** The video went viral, showcasing the power of humor and a unique selling proposition. Dollar Shave Club gained widespread attention and quickly amassed subscribers.

1. **PewDiePie (Felix Kjellberg):**

- **Approach:** PewDiePie, a top YouTuber, built his massive following by creating entertaining and relatable gaming content. He often collaborates with other creators and engages with his audience through vlogs and meme reviews.

- **Impact:** PewDiePie's success illustrates the importance of consistent content creation, understanding your audience, and adapting to trends. He has also effectively monetized his channel through sponsorships and merchandise.

1. **Nike:**

   - **Approach:** Nike utilizes YouTube for various marketing campaigns, including high-quality promotional videos and athlete endorsements. They often tell compelling stories that resonate with their target audience.

   - **Impact:** Nike's YouTube channel reinforces its brand image and values, connecting emotionally with viewers. For example, their "Just Do It" campaign has become iconic and synonymous with the brand.

1. **Casey Neistat:**

   - **Approach:** Casey Neistat, a popular vlogger and filmmaker, creates content that blends storytelling, adventure, and daily life. He has collaborated with brands for sponsored content while maintaining authenticity.

   - **Impact:** Neistat's success highlights the importance of storytelling and creating content that resonates with your audience. Brands benefit from his ability to seamlessly integrate sponsored content into his videos without alienating viewers.

1. **Red Bull:**

   - **Approach:** Red Bull is known for its extreme sports and adventure-related content. The brand sponsors and produces high-quality videos featuring stunts, events, and athlete profiles.

   - **Impact:** Red Bull's YouTube channel has become a hub for adrenaline junkies. The content aligns with their "gives you wings" slogan, creating a lifestyle brand that goes beyond just selling energy drinks.

1. **T-Series:**

   - **Approach:** T-Series, an Indian music label and film production company, has become one of the most subscribed YouTube channels globally. They upload a vast array of Bollywood music videos and film trailers.

   - **Impact:** The success of the T-Series highlights YouTube's global reach. They've effectively tapped into the entertainment preferences of a massive audience, showcasing the platform's potential for international content.

1. **Unbox Therapy (Lewis Hilsenteger):**

   - **Approach:** Unbox Therapy is a tech-focused YouTube channel where Lewis reviews and unboxes various gadgets and tech products. The content is engaging and often features the latest and most innovative tech.

   - **Impact:** Unbox Therapy has gained a massive following by providing in-depth reviews and entertainingly showcasing new tech. Brands benefit from product features and endorsements on this platform.

1. **Squarespace:**

- **Approach:** Squarespace, a website-building platform, uses YouTube for educational content. They create tutorials and guides on website design, catering to small businesses and individuals looking to create an online presence.

- **Impact:** Squarespace's YouTube strategy positions them as not just a product but as a resource. By offering valuable content, they attract users interested in website building and design, ultimately converting them into customers.

1. **Zoe Sugg (Zoella):**

   - **Approach:** Zoella, a popular lifestyle vlogger and beauty influencer, creates content ranging from fashion and beauty to personal vlogs. She often collaborates with brands for sponsored content seamlessly integrated into her videos.

   - **Impact:** Zoella's success lies in her relatable and authentic content. Brands benefit from her ability to connect with her audience and influence purchasing decisions in the beauty and lifestyle space.

These examples showcase the versatility of YouTube as a marketing platform, accommodating various niches and strategies. Successful YouTube marketing involves understanding the audience, creating compelling content, and often embracing creativity and authenticity.

Extracting Lessons and Best Practices from Successful Campaigns

YouTube marketing can be a powerful tool for businesses and creators to reach a wide audience. Analyzing successful campaigns on YouTube can provide valuable lessons and best practices. Here are some key takeaways:

1. **Know Your Audience:**
   - Successful YouTube campaigns start with a deep understanding of the target audience. Create content that resonates with your audience's interests, needs, and preferences.

1. **Compelling Thumbnails and Titles:**
   - Thumbnails and titles are the first things users notice. Create eye-catching thumbnails and compelling titles to grab attention and encourage clicks. Make sure they accurately represent the content.

1. **Quality Content is Key:**
   - High-quality, engaging content is essential. Invest in good production values, storytelling, and entertainment. Consider the format that best suits your message, whether it's tutorials, reviews, vlogs, or other types of content.

1. **Consistent Branding:**
   - Maintain a consistent brand image across your YouTube channel. Use consistent colors, logos, and messaging to build brand recognition. This helps establish trust and a sense of reliability.

1. **Optimize for Search:**
   - Utilize SEO best practices to make your videos discoverable. Include relevant keywords in video titles, descriptions, and tags. Research trending topics and incorporate them into your content when relevant.

1. **Engage with the Community:**
   - Foster a sense of community by responding to comments, asking for feedback, and encouraging viewers to like, share, and subscribe. Engaging with your audience helps build a loyal following.

1. **Collaborate with Influencers:**
   - Partnering with influencers or other creators can expand your reach. Collaborations can introduce your content to new audiences and provide a fresh perspective for your existing viewers.

1. **Utilize Cards and End Screens:**
   - Use YouTube's features like cards and end screens to encourage viewers to take action, such as watching another video, subscribing, or visiting your website. These tools can help increase user engagement and retention.

1. **Analytics and Data:**
   - Regularly analyze your YouTube analytics to understand what works and what doesn't. Track metrics such as watch time, click-through rates, and audience retention. Use this data to refine your strategy and content.

1. **Promote Off-Platform:**
   - Share your YouTube videos on other social media platforms, your website, and in email newsletters. Cross-promotion helps drive traffic to your channel and can attract a broader audience.

1. **Adapt to Trends:**
   - Stay current with YouTube trends and adapt your content accordingly. Pay attention to what's popular in

your niche and incorporate relevant trends to keep your content fresh and appealing.

1. **Create Playlists:**
   - Organize your content into playlists to make it easier for viewers to navigate your channel. Playlists encourage users to watch multiple videos simultaneously, increasing watch time.

1. **Embrace Storytelling:**
   - Storytelling is a powerful way to connect with your audience emotionally. Craft narratives that resonate with viewers evoke emotions and keep them engaged throughout the video.

1. **Mobile Optimization:**
   - Given the prevalence of mobile users, ensure your videos are optimized for mobile viewing. Test how your content appears on various devices to guarantee a positive user experience across platforms.

1. **Create Compelling Intros:**
   - Capture viewers' attention from the start with engaging intros. Clearly communicate what the video is about and why it's worth watching. Avoid lengthy intros that might discourage viewers.

1. **Call-to-Action (CTA):**
   - Include a CTA in your videos, guiding viewers on what action to take next. A strong CTA can drive user engagement whether subscribing, liking, commenting, or visiting a website.

1. **Utilize YouTube Ads:**
   - Leverage YouTube advertising to reach a broader audience. YouTube offers various ad formats,

including skippable, non-skippable, and display ads, allowing you to tailor your approach based on your campaign goals.

1. **Monitor Trends in Your Niche:**

   - Stay informed about trends within your niche. Creating content around trending topics can attract more viewers, as people often search for the latest and most relevant information.

1. **Educational Content:**

   - Provide value to your audience through educational content. Tutorials, how-to guides, and informative videos can establish your expertise in your industry and build credibility with your audience.

1. **Host Live Streams:**

   - Live streaming allows for real-time interaction with your audience. Consider hosting Q&A sessions, live events, or behind-the-scenes content to foster a sense of community and immediacy.

1. **Test and Iterate:**

   - Don't be afraid to experiment with different video formats, styles, and topics. Use A/B testing to identify what resonates best with your audience, and continually iterate based on the performance data you gather.

1. **Understand YouTube's Algorithm:**

   - Stay informed about changes in YouTube's algorithm. Understanding how the platform recommends content can help you tailor your strategy to maximize visibility and reach a wider audience.

1. **Create Evergreen Content:**

- While timely content is important, create evergreen content that remains relevant over time. This type of content can continue to attract views and engagement long after its initial release.

1. **Capitalize on Seasonal Trends:**

   - Align your content with seasonal events, holidays, or trends. This can tap into the increased interest and search activity during specific periods, giving your videos a potential boost in visibility.

1. **Optimize Video Length:**

   - While there's no one-size-fits-all rule, be mindful of video length. Some content may perform well in shorter formats, while others may benefit from more in-depth exploration. Analyze audience retention data to find the optimal length for your content.

By incorporating these additional lessons and best practices into your YouTube marketing strategy, you can enhance your chances of creating compelling, engaging content that resonates with your target audience and drives positive results.

CHAPTER 14: FUTURE TRENDS IN YOUTUBE MARKETING

Predictions and Insights into the Evolving YouTube Landscape

1. **Short-Form Video Dominance:** Short-form videos, popularized by platforms like TikTok and Instagram Reels, were gaining traction. YouTube Shorts was also emerging as a contender. Short-form content might continue to dominate in the future, with creators adapting to the trend to capture viewers' attention with limited periods.

2. **Livestreaming Growth:** Livestreaming was already on the rise, offering a more immediate and interactive way for creators to engage with their audience. The trend may continue, with more creators incorporating live streams into their content strategy to foster real-time interaction and build a stronger community.

3. **Niche and Micro-Influencers:** Smaller, niche-focused channels were gaining significance, as audiences often prefer content that caters to specific interests. Brands might collaborate more with niche and micro-influencers, recognizing the value of targeted and engaged audiences over sheer subscriber numbers.

4. **Personalization and AI Integration:** YouTube's algorithm was becoming increasingly sophisticated, providing personalized recommendations to users. Creators and marketers might leverage AI tools to better understand and cater to their audience's preferences, ensuring their content is more discoverable and engaging.

5. **Diversification of Revenue Streams:** Creators explored various revenue streams beyond traditional ads, such as channel

memberships, merchandise sales, and crowdfunding. This trend may continue, with creators looking to diversify their income sources and reduce dependence on ad revenue alone.

6. **Increased Focus on Analytics and Data:** Creators and marketers recognized the importance of analytics and data-driven insights to better understand their audience. This trend might intensify, with creators using advanced analytics tools to refine their content strategy, optimize engagement, and track the Performance of various monetization methods.

7. **Rise of Educational Content:** Educational and tutorial content was gaining popularity. Creators and brands may continue to invest in educational content, recognizing the value of providing valuable information and insights to their audience.

8. **Virtual and Augmented Reality Integration:** While not widespread in 2022, there were discussions about the potential integration of virtual and augmented reality on YouTube. This could offer new, immersive experiences for viewers, and creators might experiment with these technologies to enhance their content.

To stay up-to-date with the evolving YouTube landscape, following industry news, monitoring platform updates, and adapting strategies based on emerging trends and audience preferences is crucial.

Preparing Your Strategy for the Future

Creating a successful YouTube marketing strategy involves planning, content creation, optimization, and engagement. Here are some key steps to prepare your strategy for the future of YouTube marketing:

1. **Understand Your Audience:**
   - Define your target audience and understand their preferences, behaviors, and interests.
   - Use analytics tools to gather insights about your current audience and adapt your strategy accordingly.

1. **Set Clear Goals:**
   - Define specific, measurable, achievable, relevant, and time-bound (SMART) goals for your YouTube channel.
   - Goals could include increasing subscribers, boosting engagement, driving website traffic, or generating leads.

1. **Create Compelling Content:**
   - Produce high-quality, engaging, and relevant content that adds value to your audience.
   - To diversify your content, experiment with various video formats such as tutorials, vlogs, interviews, and product demonstrations.

1. **Optimize for Search:**
   - Conduct keyword research to identify the terms and phrases your audience is searching for.
   - Optimize video titles, descriptions, and tags with relevant keywords to improve search visibility.

1. **Utilize Thumbnails and Titles:**
   - Design eye-catching thumbnails that accurately represent the content of your video.
   - Craft compelling titles that grab attention and encourage clicks without being misleading.

1. **Consistent Branding:**

- Maintain a consistent visual identity across your YouTube channel, including logos, colors, and overall branding.
- This helps create a recognizable brand presence and foster trust with your audience.

1. **Engage with Your Community:**
   - Respond to comments, ask for feedback, and encourage viewers to like, share, and subscribe.
   - Host live streams or Q&A sessions to interact with your audience in real time.

1. **Collaborate and Cross-Promote:**
   - Collaborate with other YouTubers or influencers in your niche to expand your reach.
   - Cross-promote content on other social media platforms to drive traffic to your YouTube channel.

1. **Stay Informed About Trends:**
   - Keep abreast of the latest trends and features on YouTube.
   - Experiment with new video formats, such as shorts, and stay informed about algorithm changes and updates.

1. **Analytics and Measurement:**
   - Regularly analyze your YouTube analytics to track the Performance of your videos.
   - Adjust your strategy based on what is working and what needs improvement.

1. **Adapt to Algorithm Changes:**
   - Stay informed about any changes to the YouTube algorithm and adjust your strategy accordingly.

- Understand the factors that influence video ranking and visibility.

1. **Invest in Ads if Appropriate:**
   - Consider utilizing YouTube ads to increase visibility and reach a broader audience.
   - Use targeting options to reach specific demographics and interests.

By incorporating these strategies, you can position your YouTube channel for success in the ever-evolving landscape of online video content. Remember that staying adaptable and open to innovation is crucial in the dynamic world of digital marketing.

Made in the USA
Monee, IL
03 November 2024

69282450R00070